In the Shade of
Kanchenjunga

Kanchenjunga dominating Darjeeling (1940)

I hope you will enjoy

In the Shade of Kanchenjunga

by

Jennifer Fox

Jennifer G Fox

BACSA

PUTNEY, LONDON

1993

Published by the British Association
for Cemeteries in South Asia (BACSA)

Secretary: Theon Wilkinson MBE
76½ Chartfield Avenue
London SW15 6HQ

ISBN 0 907799 49 3

Cover design by: Jane Fox

Typeset by: Professional Presentation, 3 Prairie Road, Addlestone, Surrey

Printed by: The Chameleon Press Ltd., 5-25 Burr Road, Wandsworth SW18 4SG

Contents

Illustrations

* Acknowledgements to British Library, Oriental & India Office Collections

Foreword

'In the shade of Kanchenjunga' is the twenty-second in a series of books about Europeans in South Asia, written by a BACSA member, published by BACSA for BACSA members with a wider public in mind and particularly those who knew Darjeeling and the tea-estates around it.

The author comes of a tea-planting family, the youngest daughter of Malcolm and Eva Betten, born within sight of Kanchenjunga on the Tukvar Tea Estate in the year of the earthquake, 1934. After some twelve idyllic childhood years on various tea gardens in the district she came to live with her aunt in Kent for her British education while Darjeeling still remained her home, and in 1954 she returned there for an extended holiday at Tukvar. This was followed by a spell at Dr. Graham's Homes in Kalimpong with the luxury of being able to go home for weekends. Although she did not keep a diary during this time she wrote long letters to her aunt which she draws on in this narrative.

Her father, Malcolm Betten, OBE, was a tea-planter in Richard Magor's firm, Williamson and Magor, and was much involved with the United Kingdom Citizens Association and in many local organisations, particularly during Partition, while her mother, Eva, was Hon. Secretary of St. Andrew's, a school set up after Partition for very small children, mostly from the tea estates. In 1956 her father was transferred to Kenya and it was on the sea trip to join her parents in Africa that the author met her husband - but that is another story!

Here is a personal account which captures some of the magic of the Hills while giving a vivid description of Darjeeling from the earliest European times to 1956. In presenting this book, BACSA feels sure it will evoke many memories amongst our members while also putting on record the kind of lives Europeans led, with their joys and tribulations somehow heightened by those magnificent yet overawing mountains.

Acknowledgements

Much of the material for this book derives from family sources: my mother's recorded memories, including the Bonnerjee's family book and back numbers of Kalimpong Homes Magazines; my father's books and papers; my own letters. My thanks for the discussions on Darjeeling to my sister Ann, a number of old family friends and to Mrs. Tassell, whose aunt's 19th century travel diary provided a stimulus.

I wish to record my gratitude to Mr. Richard Magor for lending me his office to research in the archives of Williamson & Magor and Tukvar Tea Estate and also for some personal anecdotes; the Royal Geographical Society and Messrs. Thomas Cook for use of their libraries; and The India Office Library and Records for providing many fascinating hours of research.

I would like to record my gratitude for the help I received from the late Grace Evans and the late Ronnie Bryan, at that time the Bishop of Barrackpore. I wish also to include in my thanks others who helped at various stages: Fred Pinn, John Poole and Ronald Cleaver.

Special thanks for the delightful cover design are due to my daughter-in-law, Jane; and for overall support to my long-suffering husband, Roger, without whose tolerance and encouragement this book would never have been finished.

Finally, and with much gratitude, I acknowledge the help given by Theon Wilkinson and Rosie Llewellyn-Jones in the production of the book.

Jennifer Fox

O = not on plan

viii

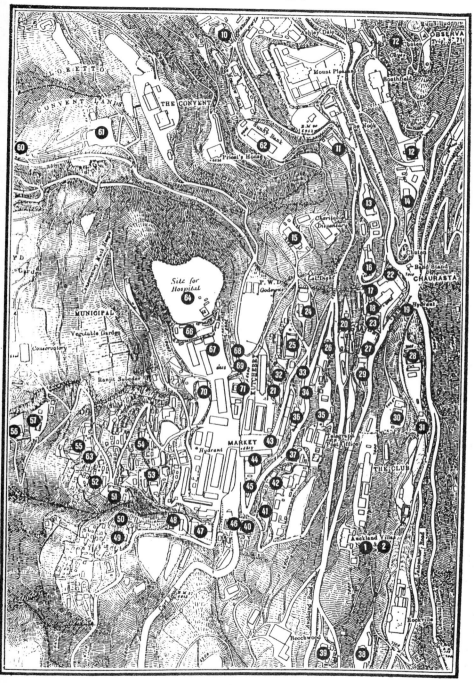

To the memory
of my parents,
Eva and Malcolm Betten

1

Introduction

The two usual ways to travel to India during the early days of the nineteenth century, when this story of British Sikkim and of Darjeeling tea begins, were either overland to the east coast of Africa and then across the Indian Ocean by sailing ship, or round the Cape of Good Hope. Incredible though it is to us today, sailing ships were even used to transport ice from America, round the Cape to Calcutta, to relieve those of the British Raj who found the heat more than they could bear. Over the years there were changes, as steam replaced sail and refrigeration the ice ships.

At the end of the nineteenth century and during the first half of this one, most of the Britons who travelled to Darjeeling went through the Suez Canal on one of the large passenger liners which docked at Bombay. Some took the slower cargo boats which also went through the Suez Canal but docked at Calcutta and were a cheaper form of travel. So when, after a pleasant sea trip in 1953 I found myself in the port of Bombay I had followed in the wake of many of my fellow countrymen and women who travelled between India and Britain during the bygone days of the British Raj. At Bombay I piled my trunks onto the Calcutta Express for the journey to Calcutta. Because the train trundled its way across a part of the Indian subcontinent this journey was scheduled to last twenty-five hours.

It was hot in Calcutta when I arrived, the sweat and the discomfort being part of the magic, the India I had come back to after an absence of seven years. Following India's Independence much had changed and much, like the heat and vast landscape, was the same. One of these changes was the next stage of my journey for when I stepped into the jostling Bengali crowd which is Calcutta station I no longer faced another overnight train journey to the foot of the Himalaya mountains, instead I caught the plane to Bagdogra.

The letters I wrote to my aunt in England tell of the heat, of a bus ride through Calcutta and the sweat at Dum Dum airport waiting for a Dakota of Indian Airways. Hot and travel weary, it was a relief to take off on time, if anything, early. As I settled into my seat, the sweat wet on my face, it was not difficult to imagine how grateful the Calcutta residents must have been for the cargoes of American ice and how eagerly they must have awaited the development of the station at Darjeeling. Sitting in my sweat-soaked dress it was easy to sympathise with Jo Calcutta's disappointment when he read of delays in establishing Darjeeling. As the problems with creating Darjeeling grew, some understanding is required of the administration's desire for a scapegoat. Had there been a better understanding of hill country and more patience, the administration might have been kinder to the man whose drive, initiative and vision did so much to create the town.

Once aboard the small plane I fastened my seat belt and looked forward, as countless had done before me, to my mountain destination and a cool breeze. I looked round the plane, the passengers were mostly hill folk, Tibetans, tall and strong, the beautiful women in their striped aprons, the Nepalese, smaller but still with Mongolian features, the women loaded with heavy necklaces and bracelets. There were also Indians, mostly wearing European dress but two Bengalis in *dhotis* and then there was myself, the only European on the plane and, although only twenty years old, belonging to a bygone era!

The plane had finished climbing and settled into a flight path which was to take us over the flood plain of the river Ganges, flying due north, over what was then East Pakistan but today is Bangladesh, towards the Himalayas, that vast two thousand mile arc of mountains which border the Indian subcontinent. The plane was heading, not only towards the world's most lofty and formidable regions, but also towards secret kingdoms and countries which, in 1953, were closed to foreigners and to the western world in particular.

The steward bought me a magazine to read, some hot coffee and excellent chicken sandwiches. I had barely finished eating when the pilot of the plane invited me into the cockpit to experience an unimaginable panorama. This gesture of Indian welcome was a much appreciated and oft remembered treat. Today as one flies here and there the world shrinks in size but that day, as I looked out of the cockpit the world took on a larger dimension. The reality is that Northern India is on the scale of the giant's land.

The day was perfect, and that distance which is the end of human sight was a hazy horizon. Because we were not flying high, we could watch the land slip past below. It was a giantscape of brown land through which Mother Ganges snaked her watery way. Two recent floods were subsiding, the rivers were brown, full of suspended silt, and murky from destruction. From the cockpit of the Dakota one got a bird's eye view of a devastation which was awesome in its expanse.

The pilot drew my attention to the horizon, at the full range of a man's eyes, hazy with the distance were the Himalayas rising out of the plains millimetre by centimetre. We flew on and shapes could be discerned, Mounts Everest and Makulu rose over Nepal while on the east side the Kanchenjunga range looked down on Sikkim, the snow line stretching round to Bhutan. Everest, twice as high as Europe's Matterhorn; Kanchenjunga seven times as high as Snowdon. The passes into the secret land of Tibet rising twice as high as the Great St. Bernard or St. Gotthardt. Not only are there 75 peaks all over 24,000 feet

(Europe's Mont Blanc is under 16,000), but the Himalayas are the source of life-giving and life-destroying water from the rivers which debouch all that is good and bad onto the plains of India and Bangladesh.

This was a sight for a giant's eyes, not for mine, for in the context of that scene a giant would have needed a powerful microscope to see the plane let alone me and he would have been more able, because he could see more of it, to appreciate the size of what lay ahead.

It is no wonder that the Himalayas impressed those whose only mode of travel was to slog the plains of Hindustan on foot and to record as one such traveller did that:

> Forty miles away is a range of hills rich in verdure, their summits covered with stately forests of saul, sissoo and fir trees, beyond which, towering high above the clouds, are the gigantic Himalaya mountains, their heads crowned with eternal snow and glittering with thousands of solar beams playing on the immense glaciers of the unexplored regions.

Today we know what is behind those mountains, then, at the beginning of the nineteenth century, the map of Central Asia was a blank. From the Pamirs to Tibet, the Gobi Desert to the Steppes of Siberia the maps were white with only a thin line to mark the route taken by Marco Polo and the old silk caravans.

Nestled somewhere in amongst the forest which the early Hindustan traveller described, and hiding amidst firs, magnolia, rhododendrons and poinsettia was Darjeeling, lying with its back to the heat, dust and disease of the plains and Calcutta. For Darjeeling faces north to mountains of mystery and legend, mountains whose size and extent defy man's comprehension.

It was a short flight and soon the plane dipped down, the snows went from view and we made a perfect landing. This journey from Calcutta had been as quick, pleasant and easy as the journey of the Loreto nuns, one hundred years before, had been hot, long, uncomfortable and from time to time frightening.

From the airport there is today, a taxi ride up to Darjeeling, an experience which many unused to mountain roads and hill drivers find exciting enough but the three hours it takes to leave the sweat and find a refreshing cup of tea is nothing compared to the sagas enacted as the first Europeans struggled into British Sikkim.

My taxi climbed up, round, in, out, and up, up beside the track of the Darjeeling Himalayan Railway. No toy train this but hailed as one of the engineering feats of the nineteenth century even if one of its most spectacular views was referred to as Agony Point.

At Dorje-ling, as it was once called, there was a short pause before the last short leg of my journey. My father was waiting at the Planters Club and while we exchanged greetings I gazed at the magnificence of the Kanchenjunga range, a mere forty miles away as the crow flies. I drew in a deep breath, the last stage of my journey was to be a hair-raising descent into an Himalayan valley and to Tukvar Tea Estate - one of the earliest tea estates to be established and the most notoriously frightening road in the district.

Today Darjeeling is known world-wide as a brand of upmarket tea with its town a name in a travel brochure and a place of refuge for the many Tibetans who came there to escape the Chinese in the 1950s.

In spite of the aura of mysticism which clings to this giant landscape, not much is known of the early history before the nineteenth century and the end of the beginning of the fighting with the Nepalese. The Tibetan Buddhist monastery was destroyed when the Nepalese built a Gurkha station during their occupation of Sikkim. The settlement made by the Nepalese was also a ruin when the first British arrived. The indigenous population, the few Lepchas, who were scattered through the forests, were once the rulers of most of the land. They have a tradition of the flood and a home on Mount Ararat.

The Tibetans built their monastery on the knoll of Darjeeling. One can see the shape of the original hill in old photographs before the houses hid it. The land on which the monastery was built is like a pillar, the Ling of Darjeeling. The Tibetans did not build at the summit, on what is today's Tiger Hill, the highest point above Darjeeling, as one might have expected because it is cold and too wet for comfort. The tor, or knoll, on which this monastery was built rises above the general line of the hill, rather like a wart would rise above the nose of a giant. By the site is a cave and a natural tunnel into the rock which is said to lead to the very heart of the mountains, right to Lhasa and the Dalai Lama. Like the air passages from the giant's nose lead to his lungs and his heart and like the giant has various passages, arteries and windpipes so the Sikkim mountains contain caves and tunnels, which, to my knowledge, have not been fully explored. I visited one almost inaccessible cave which had several entrances and tunnels and although the party wore climbing boots and carried ropes we were unable to explore beyond the second cavern. The myth that the Darjeeling cave has a direct link, a kind of 'hot line' to Lhasa is one I like to foster.

'Dorje', today's Darj has been given several meanings but only two will be considered now. It is generally accepted that 'sceptre' or 'Holy Place' is the meaning, but when the earth quakes, when thunder roars through the deep valleys and the hills are lit by almost continuous lightning, Darj is once again the place of the thunderbolt.

'Ling' also has several meanings, one is quite simply 'place', place of the sceptre or of the thunderbolt. The other, more realistic translation is a pillar, either to commemorate a battle or some other important occurrence.

From Darjeeling's early days there has been a monument or *chorten* to mark the site of both the ruined monastery and the sacred ground, sacred to the presence of Mahakal Baba, who is worshipped as a divine manifestation. This holy monument or *chorten* gives a particularly Tibetan flavour to this corner of Asia which was once British Sikkim.

Chortens are found all over the mountains of Sikkim as well as in Tibet, many are small and insignificant, but set amongst the Himalayas they give form and atmosphere to a landscape which is huge, beautiful and savagely cruel. All *chortens* are a reminder of the cosmic drama, of the perpetual cycle of birth and re-birth and of the wheel of life. An interpretation for the symbolic structure of the *chorten* is that it represents a miniature of lamaist cosmology. The base of the structure represents earth, the tower represents water and one of the two objects at the top stand for air and the atmosphere, an inverted vault of heaven. The other object at the top is the sun, a flame, to symbolise space, ether, the most subtle of the elements. *Chortens* will contain the ashes or bones of a venerated lama, sacred pictures or writings.

Beside the Darjeeling *chorten* flutter prayer flags. As perpetual as the breath of life these flags tell their prayers and as the breeze or the wind blows so they continuously are wafting their prayers over the hills and valleys and, in the case of Darjeeling, over the streets of the town. The most important prayer, the one found written on rocks, by waterfalls, in inaccessible places is the one most oft repeated 'Om mani padme hum', 'hail oh jewel in the flower of the lotus'.

The following pages cover the period from around 1820 through to 1957, a century after the first tea bush was raised from seed and a decade after India's Independence which makes a natural break because the Darjeeling British left slowly with no natural cut off point while the flood of Tibetan refugees into the district marks a firm beginning of a new period.

Being the daughter of a British tea planter I have, inevitably, given a Raj flavour to this history. But it is hoped that time and experience has tempered the perspective into something approaching reality rather than bias. That said, it has to be remembered that any work which has such a personal association is more of an interpretation, than a scholastic work.

It is not the intention to condone British rule in India but to state facts which concern both British Sikkim and the tea industry because to appreciate Darjeeling and its famous teas one needs to know something of its history and its weather because they are all part of the subtle flavour and aroma of Darjeeling tea.

This is not intended to be a detailed textbook study but a perception of a town's development, including extracts from early pioneers and some personal comments from time to time. Men and women of the numerous races who made Darjeeling their home will have a different interpretation on the facts and have access to their own source information. Others would not give so much space to Tibet, that kingdom across the mountains, but it is the writer's opinion that the town, facing as it does, north towards the passes into that 'secret' kingdom must be influenced by its affairs.

And the mountains, one cannot talk of Darjeeling and forget the mountains. Mount Everest, seen from Darjeeling's Tiger Hill at sunrise is, today, the highlight of the traveller's visit and a challenge to every mountaineer, but in 1836 the mountain had still to be 'discovered'. There are also the people of the mountains, the Gurkhas, world famous for bravery, the Bhutanese, Lepchas and Tibetans, the Nepalese and the Sherpas to mention but a few of Darjeeling's cosmopolitan society, many of whom have made their way into the pages of world history. We begin with the creation of Darjeeling and with the then Raja of Sikkim and his Prime Minister whose generosity, intrigue and cunning, flavour the early pages of this story.

A chorten with prayer-flags

2

The Decision to Create Darjeeling is Made

The East India Company responded to the frequent requests of both Mr. Grant and Captain Lloyd that Darjeeling be a sanatorium by sending Captain Herbert the Deputy Surveyor-General 'to explore the tracts of the Sikkim hills with Mr. Grant'. Their reports of this exploration were dated 20th and 21st April 1830 and Captain Herbert's report was, on the whole, enthusiastic.

Captain Herbert considered that Darjeeling, being deserted, could only improve and that part of the ridge, called Ging, a little below Darjeeling had, even in its neglected state, a great natural beauty while the view of the snowy range from Senchal mountain must be one of the most magnificent in the world and included the peak of 'Kunching Junga said to be 27,000 ft above sea and supposed by some to be a volcano'.

He described the interior of Sikkim as being 'an accumulation of very steep mountains separated by deep abysses so narrow at the bottom in general as to scarcely allow room for the torrent which rushes along it'. Captain Herbert recorded that the mountain sides were usually steepest at the valley bottom where they appeared almost perpendicular.

Because the Calcutta residents were so desperate to have a refuge from the heat, Captain Herbert felt that a mere 98 hours spent on the road from Calcutta was no inconvenience. Furthermore there was water travel to within 60 miles of the hills possible all the year round and to within 30 miles during June to September. Travel by river steamer was slower but more comfortable. The town of Allahabad was 400 miles in a direct line to Darjeeling and it was, therefore, considered that all stations south of Allahabad would find Darjeeling a better place for a sanatorium than Simla.

To begin with, of course, all foodstuffs such as grain and animal feeds would have to come from the plains, but Captain Herbert considered that this was no great problem since the mountains would 'soon be self sufficient even to the extent of supplying all the European population of India...' In no parts of the world were such pastures to be found as was proved by the excellent condition of the cattle. Sheep, too, could be profitable using the fine breed of Tibetan sheep which produced excellent wool.

Lack of a labour force was not an argument since there would be a large influx of poor people from Nepal, many of whom had once lived on the hill sides and who had taken refuge from the Raja of Sikkim. Since these people would clear the forest as necessary, there would only be some long grass to be cut before building could begin. There would be no problem in clearing the area required for the town of forest because firewood and building timber would quickly 'eat into the immediate forest'.

Mr. Grant was of the opinion that the station of Darjeeling was healthy because of the 'ruddiness of complexion of the hill people' and that some lived to a hundred years and Captain Herbert reported that unlike other sites he had visited such as Almorah, there was no problem with water as there were good springs at Darjeeling with a supply of good, healthy water.

Furthermore with a road made passable through Sikkim, the Bhutias would open up trade between themselves, Darjeeling, Bengal and even Chinese Tartary and Mr. Grant had been assured that there were excellent flocks of sheep in the mountains. Perhaps just a guard would be needed at the River Teesta!

It was reported that there were some wild animals, several species of deer, hog, antelope and wild goat, pheasant, partridge and types of quail and some of the birds, like the chikor could be easily tamed.

To support his claim that the journey from Calcutta was no problem the Captain had logged his journey, the number of hours each stage had taken and the length of each rest. He had left Calcutta on 6th February 1830 at 7 am and arrived at Delamcotta Stockade on the 13th at 2 pm. He travelled for 98 hours at an average speed of three and a quarter miles an hour thus making Delamcotta an estimated 319 miles from Calcutta with just the 8,000 feet climb into the hills to come.

The journey was not anticipated to be particularly unhealthy, though, in Captain Herbert's opinion, the 'Teruaee' or Terai could be a problem and it should be noted that the meaning of the word is moist. Travellers must not linger on this section of the journey as the untimely death of the beautiful Lady Canning, who stopped to paint, was later to prove. Herbert did not consider the actual forest itself to be unhealthy because it was on well drained soil and on a shelving bank of gravel and sand. (Even as late as 1830, fever, that rather loose word used to cover disease, was as dread and mortal as cholera or dysentery. It was not until 1880 that the malarial parasites were discovered in blood cells and not until Ronald Ross, working in India, between 1897 and 1899 that the part mosquitoes play in malaria began to be understood.)

It was recommended that Titalya, in the plains, could be the point of departure for Darjeeling and thereafter there be only one road although Grant talks of three original 'roads' leading to Darjeeling, two by the Nagri Pass and a third by the Mahananda. The latter he describes as being deserted and overgrown with jungle. The route via the Nagri Pass to Senchal had the advantage of being direct but the snag of being impassable in rainy weather, while the other by the Sabbok Golah was also a dry weather route, more circuitous and more rugged. It has to be noted that Mr. Grant used the word 'road' for want of a more suitable term.

Mr. Grant's report suggested that a road could be built a few miles from the Nagri Pass at Russudhora where the river Balasun breaks into two streams and where a ridge commences to rise gradually until joining the southern base of Senchal. This route would have the advantage of reaching a cool climate quickly, the temperature falling by one degree for every three hundred feet climbed and, in Grant's opinion, 'reaching a cool climate was worth almost any sacrifice'. Mr. Grant also suggested that once Titalya was left travellers should not stop until they had reached the hills.

Darjeeling was, it must be remembered, still part of that territory which the East India Company had restored to the Sikkim Raja at the end of the Nepalese war. Although there followed a delay of several years, the final decision took a mere two minutes of Lord William Bentinck's time and the establishment of the sanatorium was more than a dream even if the reality of it was to be a nightmare to some. The first step was to acquire the land. It would appear that although the Governor General had agreed to Darjeeling either he or his advisors, or both, were not fully convinced of the viability of Darjeeling and were not prepared to involve the Company in too much expense for its acquisition. The people of Calcutta were putting pressure on them for a sanatorium and Darjeeling was, on the face of it, the only possible choice, but that another better site might or could be found, must have always been in their minds.

However matters progressed and Colonel Lloyd, who was most enthusiastic for Darjeeling was asked to negotiate with the Raja at an auspicious moment.

The incursion of various Lepchas from Nepal who had taken refuge from Sikkim gave the opportunity of a visit to the Sikkim Raja, and Colonel Lloyd was able to meet the Raja and return with the unconditional cession of the uninhabited mountain of Darjeeling.

At first the Sikkim Raja had wished to exchange Darjeeling for some fertile land, the Debange, which had been conferred in perpetuity to the Raja of Jalpaiguri and Begampur in 1828 as compensation for injuries. That being out of the question the Raja then agreed to hand over the uninhabited Darjeeling. The Raja's deed of grant is dated 1st February 1835 and reads as follows:

> The Governor General, having expressed his desire for possession of the hill of Darjeeling on account of its cool climate, for the purpose of enabling the servants of his Government, suffering from sickness, to avail themselves of its advantages, I, the Sikkimputtee Rajah, out of friendship for the said Governor General, hereby present Darjeeling to the East India Company, that is, all the land South of the Great Rangit river, East of the Balasun, Kahail and Little Rangit rivers and West of Rungno and Mahanadi rivers.

It is possible that the Sikkim Raja was bemused, possibly even suspicious of the British request for the hill of Darjeeling, not only because it was more or less uninhabited but also because, in his opinion it was too damp. The climate at Darjeeling was wetter than that of much of Sikkim and Rinchenpong in particular. Moreover, the Raja was a Tibetan and as such he preferred to live in Tibet's Chumbi valley where the climate was the more to his taste. He cannot have put much value on Darjeeling and could have seen his gift as little more than a friendly, political gesture. From his future actions, it is clear, however, that either he had changed his mind about his generous gift or he felt he had not received an adequate 'present' in return. Mention is made of pearls and corals and other gifts which were not forthcoming from the British in Calcutta!

The Court of Directors of the East India Company did not give the go-ahead for Darjeeling to be built. They were still not convinced that building a station on the land called Dorje-ling was a viable proposition. No houses were allowed to be built, no land sold or allocated, and Colonel Lloyd was again sent to make a more thorough investigation of the general possibilities of the place before considering any financial contribution.

In July 1836 Captain Surgeon H. Chapman was directed to go to Titalya and put himself under the orders of Lieutenant Colonel Lloyd and to accompany that gentleman to Darjeeling in the Sikkim mountains. Dr. Chapman was known personally to the Court of Directors, and his impressions were, therefore, more valuable to the Court of Directors of the East India Company than those of old campaigners such as Grant and Lloyd. Although he left Calcutta on 14th August there was much to be done at Titalya before they were ready to leave for Darjeeling in November and as it was, Colonel Lloyd, ever impatient to get on with the job, made him leave before a consignment of special instruments had arrived from Calcutta and he had no alternative but to manage without.

Colonel Lloyd and Dr. Chapman left Titalya early on the morning of 11th November 1836 but at midday had to halt as the road was no longer suitable for the elephant and the carriages (loaded wagons). These were sent back and the party proceeded on foot. The distance of the first day's march was so short that Lloyd had hoped that the hundred coolies, whom he had enrolled as porters, would manage two trips with the provisions but right from the start he was to experience delays and frustrations added to which the jungle frequently had to be cut back from the 'road' to make it wide enough for the coolies and their burdens.

There was also trouble with their porters. Just one day out from Titalya on 12th November Chapman recorded in his journal 'we were much inconvenienced this morning for want of coolies, many of the men we brought with us from Titalaya absconded during the night.'

Most of their problems were due to the Sikkim Raja who wished he had not given Darjeeling away and wanted to prevent them getting there. His tactics were to put such fear into the local Lepchas that without the aid of porters the plans for Darjeeling would have to be abandoned. Instead of relying on the hillmen Lloyd had to recruit plainsmen as porters. When these ploys of the Raja did not work a letter was sent to Lloyd warning him not to proceed but as the Colonel wrote in his journal 'it was in the Bhutia language and all Greek to me!' The Doctor's journal, on the other hand made no bones about the fact that the Sikkim Raja had threatened that the Nepalese would cut their throats if they proceeded to Darjeeling, but he continues more hopefully 'Road from Tikribong was in tolerably good order, not so difficult as in past marches.'

Chapman had not enjoyed the early part of the march. He described Dimaligolah as a place with 'a few odd huts standing which are annually repaired by the Lepchas which are used by Bengalis and hill people to barter. It is a horrible spot, surrounded by grass and jungle and enclosed by hills with no ventilation. Two men are ill with intermittent fever and more will be if we remain here many days. Weather overcast and because of jungle can see nothing of surrounding country.'

He refers to slow progress, gigantic trees and a perpendicular path. The path was rough, rocky and uneven and they crossed the river Balasun by a crude bridge of bamboos laid from rock to rock and were travelling along the bed of the river through unhealthy country and tall jungle grass.

However, Goolia Muni was a 'romantic spot with river running close under lofty perpendicular mountains on the righthand side.' The river was deep and full of fish. But the Balasun had to be crossed three times more on that march making it 'a most fatiguing day'.

Their problems did not decrease as they climbed higher though the path did improve. Because of their problems with the Sikkim Raja they were employing plainsmen as porters and these men were not adequately dressed for the colder temperatures they were experiencing. Chapman recorded that Tikribong, at 5,159 feet was cold but they went on up to Oong Gool. Chapman wrote:

very steep, on gaining the top a most magnificent view of the Snowy Range. Coolies ran off. Two more sepoys and several of our porters attacked with fever, the weather cloudy and very chilly. Last night was 42 and this morning 40 deg. We march for Darjeeling tomorrow.

The following extracts from Colonel Lloyd's journal show some of the problems that they had with the porters:

80 loads carried by 102 men despatched to the Golah this morning. After the arrival of the coolies this morning 165 wrote names down but too late to send them off so they cut bamboos and built houses in which to store grain. Sent on Chaprassi and two Lepchas to endeavour to erect a hut at Pandong for grain.

141 coolies despatched with loads to Pandong with orders to return in the evening having left their loads. These people have such a habit of sitting down to smoke on the road that I fear I shall not be obeyed. The distance is not more than six miles.

11

...we sent on the Lepchas with orders to clear a spot on which a tent could be pitched at Pandong and followed them up ourselves, ascending and descending about fifteen ravines and water courses till we came into the bed of the Balasun and crossed that river three times more. A very tedious march of four hours 40 minutes. The Lepchas we had sent on were clearing a space for my tent and I got them to erect a hut for Doctor Chapman after which they were quite satisfied at receiving a bottle of brandy and salt.

9 coolies reported sick today, only half coolies returned and 9 deserted during the night.

The coolies sent on to clear the road but having met eight or nine Lepchas coming down the hill they returned without doing so but took care not to come in till the evening so they would not be sent out again. One day has thus been lost. Coolies sent off under Sirdar to clear road. Until this has been done banghys cannot be carried. They returned in the evening having made a path to Tikribong and as the Lepchas have cleared the other half I shall march tomorrow.

On 1st December, the Colonel and the Doctor reached Darjeeling with no guard and no coolies. On December 2nd Lloyd wrote in his journal:

No dinner and no bed yesterday - luckily there was a Lepcha house which had been built last May by the order of the Raja at my request. We passed the night in it sitting round a fire but were still cold and uncomfortable. The ground was this morning covered with hoar frost. The coolies and guard made their appearance about 9 o'clock. They had stopped within fifteen minutes walk from us and I expect for no reason other than to smoke for they had no excuse to offer for not having come on last evening. There are a few Lepchas here sent by the Raja, they had constructed huts for us. More durable habitations must be made. Mr. Chapman has agreed with these men to make him a hut which he can reside in. They are also to make a habitation for me.

The Lepchas were expert at making overnight accommodation or huts, it would take one man less than an hour to build and furnish a hut but obviously Lloyd and Chapman wished for something more substantial for their stay in Darjeeling.

December 3. The coolies were divided into two parties one of which was to clear the ground and erect huts for the people. The other was despatched to bring up supplies from Tikribong, allowing them one day to go and one to come back.

Monday 12 December - As the coolies have to-day completed their month and have no food remaining I am under necessity of allowing them to return to the plains for the purpose of providing food and clothing and advancing them one month's pay at Rupees 4 a month and it is with considerable difficulty that I induce them to take with that amount, if I could have procured Lepchas and Bhutias I would not have consented to give more than Rupees 3.... The coolies are to return by 25th with one month's food for each man. Instead of hiring 200 men I have selected 100 of the strongest and the hardiest among them.

29 December 1836 - The coolies returned this day number 92, I sent 40 from the station to bring up more supplies, divided into groups of ten at the various stopping places on the way up with finally 10 at Oong Gool above Tikribong. The remaining 52 are to be kept here to clear jungle, form a reservoir from the spring and do various jobs which are required by the way of erecting huts etc.

Tuesday 10 January. This morning at daylight it commenced snowing, thunder and lightning and by noon the snow was one foot deep (this was later found to be exceptionally deep for Darjeeling). It has, of course, put a stop to all work. The coolies are wretchedly off for want of clothing. If the snow had gone on they must have deserted. The Lepcha Vakeel, sent by the Sikkim Raja, who made their appearance yesterday have been obliged to go down to beyond Ging for they had not sufficient shelter where they were bivouacked.

Large body of Lepchas arrived from the plains bringing up goods for the Sikkim Raja, well inclined to be troublesome.

Chapman has less to say of his arrival at Darjeeling:

December 1 - Tikribong to Darjeeling. A fine clear morning. 7 a.m. Arrived Darjeeling at 1.30 - 9 miles. Huts at Darjeeling erected by order of Raja, one of which spent we a wretched night in, no coolies had arrived, we had neither food nor bedding.

Short distance back the next morning we found coolies round a fire, bright frosty morning - water frozen.

December 22nd - morning cloudy and moist - afternoon clear. Several Bhotias arrived today on way to the Ganges - they are dirty wretches. The Lama paid me a visit today and showed great curiosity, he was much intrigued with the microscope, the camera and other things which I showed him.

Back in Calcutta the newspapers were following all that was going on in Darjeeling with great interest. Although the *Friend of India* in Calcutta was happy to record the temperature in Darjeeling it is surprising, in view of that publication's pre-occupation with the 'ice problem' that no one speculated, then, of the possibility of transporting ice down the Himalayas instead of across the oceans. Once railways were being built, however, they did suggest that a line should be taken up to 14,000 feet into the mountains to enable ice to be transported down to Calcutta.

In Calcutta, the weather during June 1837 was hotter than ever and cholera was bad. The pressure for the hill station of Darjeeling increased with every upward movement of the thermometer.

Rock-cutting - mile 29

3

A Journey and a Half

Lloyd spent a year in Darjeeling. His last job was to cut the line for the road to link Titalya with Darjeeling beginning at Oong Ghool. In the journal that he kept we learn not only of the hills in which he was working but also more of the man himself. He had a vision for Darjeeling and a country full of problems or infested with tigers was unimportant. He did not regard the jungle as impenetrable. He makes a casual reference to the fact that the hills were infested with tigers, there was no mention of leopards but plenty of deer and antelope. He recorded the long jungle grass and of the forest said, 'the trees are not close and the undergrowth consists of brambles and various ground creepers which though they impeded our progress on foot cannot cause any obstacles. In short, no mountain country could be more favourable for a road.'

At first it looked as if there was progress. It was decided to develop the site as a sanatorium and Lloyd, now General Lloyd was appointed a Local Agent to deal with applications for land, of which there was no shortage, from the Calcutta residents. But there were problems and Lloyd's name disappears, hidden by archive dust and a new one appears.

In 1839 Dr. Campbell of the Indian Medical Service and the British Resident in Nepal was transferred to Darjeeling as Superintendent and to be in charge of political relations with Sikkim. By 1841 a road, following Lloyd's line had been built from Pankhabari, where there was a staging bungalow. There was another staging bungalow, a quite appalling one, at Mahaldiram and this was later abandoned; a hotel was built en route at Kurseong with another at Darjeeling (though the word 'hotel' is something of an euphemism) and thirty private houses had been built, with other sites taken up.

The glowing reports of Darjeeling which the Calcutta residents had received, quite naturally led them to begin packing their bags in readiness for their holidays and when reports of delays came in they were aghast and furious. No one, least of all Jo Calcutta had any understanding of the problems that faced the Darjeeling builders.

It would not be difficult, Lloyd was sure, to make a road from the plains to Darjeeling and he even talked of carriages from time to time, not just a road for cattle and foot traffic. There were many technical problems to be overcome. No one had built roads into mountains such as these before and many regarded the reality of building the road to Darjeeling a nightmare. One should not ridicule

15

Lloyd's optimism nor the problems and difficulties faced by those inexperienced in mountain road building. This is not a saga on the road to Darjeeling.

Let it just be said that apart from the basic problem of engineering a road into the mountains when nearly every inch of the way had to be cut by dynamite into the cliff side for mile after tedious mile, there was the problem of labour, acquiring labour, housing labour, feeding labour and keeping labour. They were working in forested, mountainous country miles from civilisation. No wonder that the illnesses of the first engineer appointed to do the job were considered to be psychosomatic. No sooner was a stretch of road made than it was made impassable by mud or landslips caused by the monsoon. It is not easy to ascertain just how much of the basic donkey-work had been done by the time that Lieutenant Napier was appointed to the Darjeeling Road but the fact is that Napier was an energetic and capable man who was to rise to the peerage before the end of his career and was quickly to create the road to Darjeeling.

Without a reasonable road it was impossible for all the food, furniture and general necessities for building a town to be carried up the 7,000 feet into the mountains. And with no facilities for the porters and no adequate track how could progress at the sanatorium be made?

Even today the journey to Darjeeling can make a good story with which to entertain less adventurous friends but to have ever suggested, as Herbert and others did, that it was not much more than an afternoon stroll was misleading. No wonder that there were problems in getting the town established. As the reports filtered back to Calcutta it looked as if only those with the toughness and determination of the lunatic would be able to complete the journey. The first problem was to reach the foot of the mountains, that being done there was a fair chance one would survive the climb out of the heat for every step one took one was encouraged on by the cooling temperature.

In one of the earliest reports, Captain Herbert described Darjeeling as being a mere 98 hours by dawk from Calcutta, implying that it was no distance and no trouble! Travelling dawk meant one travelled by *palkee*, at night; each staging post was 12 miles and the bearers averaged, if their torches did not go out, just over three miles an hour. The *palkee* was little better than a coffin; since one could sit up in it and it was open at one side it was, perhaps, slightly better. This thing was carried by men.

Darjeeling had, however, been proved to be such a splendid place to restore the sick to health that the Catholic Archbishop Carew determined that a group of Calcutta's Loreto nuns establish two schools there, one for boys and one for girls.

He wished two nuns to go up by dawk-palanquin to see for themselves assuming that there would be no problem in covering four hundred miles of dust-tracks, crossing three hundred bridges and sleeping in the vehicles. Fortunately for the nuns Judge Loughnan was consulted and was horrified at the prospect and

16

pointed out that since the Darjeeling residents could be counted on one hand there really was no need for schools. But the Archbishop was determined and instead of two sent a party of five young women with a chaplain to travel by river craft as far as Kisanganj. This would enable them to make use of the hospitality which would be offered to them along the way.

A prospectus was published and a public loan opened to finance the scheme. On 10th August 1846 the young women, dressed in the thick black habit of their order, left Calcutta with quantities of luggage. Not only were they to be seven weeks on the river but there would be another eleven days in the jungle and then on arrival they had to furnish their house, a chapel and two schools. They needed a lot of luggage!

The river journey was always 'interesting' and progress up the Ganges, travelling against the current was slow and dependent on favourable winds. In the early stages there was the force of the flood tide to help but more often than not progress depended on the rowing ability and stamina of the crew. Then there were stretches when the boats were dragged up by tow-line. It was a long 200 miles.

In the wet season stretches of Bengal might appear, from river level, almost like an inland sea. The rice is under water, in August not yet showing its green tips. There is no work in the fields, and the villager, who was out to collect field-crabs or set his fish trap, stands waist-deep in water. Days of muggy heat, days of driving rain, days when the leaden sky hung heavily over the grey expanse of waters, till a flash and sudden growl of thunder sent the little raft hurrying to the bank before a storm over took them. The food on board could not have been very good. I hope they knew enough to vary it by an occasional purchase of mangoes or bananas, or a basket of rosy lichis. There was hardly room to stretch their legs on deck, yet when they drew in to the banks, at evening, the mud roads of the villages were quagmires, and the smell of the cooking in mustard oil was not too pleasant a variation from the 'unforgettable unforgotten river smell' that was their atmosphere. Night often brought no relief from the stifling heat, only an incredible increase of insect life.

They did not always have to sleep on board as the promised bungalows did from time to time materialise - as one they stayed at:

This was the residence of Mr. Barnes, a wealthy timber merchant, indigo planter and zemindar, or big land-owner, of Boornie, and the brother-in-law of Judge Loughnan. It was their first introduction to the kind of home a retired civil servant or prosperous tea planter builds for himself in the Darjeeling district, the 'bungalow' from which many of their future pupils were to come.

It is with this little party of nuns that we first meet Mr. Perry the District Magistrate at Kisanganj. Two years later he was to assist Joseph Hooker with his travel problems. In fact one must wonder whether his whole time was not to assist the unfortunates on the journey to Darjeeling! The nuns stayed with Mr. Perry for several days while their luggage was assembled and preparations made for the next stage of their journey. For this they hired six palkees, seventy-four palkee bearers and a form of transport that looked like bullock-carts but had no bullocks. These were 'push-pushes' and had high matting roofs, no springs and no tyres and were propelled by manpower, four men at the shafts with two or four pushing from behind.

Pleased to be on the last leg of this long journey the party of young women were blissfully ignorant of their bearers' preoccupation with a tiger's pugmarks in the road. Suddenly with a cry of 'bagh! bagh!' tiger, tiger, the bearers were off and the nuns left abandoned to pull up their shutters, grasp their rosaries and pray. Eventually the frightened bearers returned and they were able to resume their journey.

They arrived in Darjeeling on 10th October to set up house in one of two cottages. Their neighbour was a Christian of the Protestant persuasion and so grimly did she view her Sabbath that even her hens were kept locked up until Monday lest they disturb the atmosphere of prayer. One can imagine with what amusement the other residents viewed the arrival of the nuns and their noisy Sunday choir practice. But she found, to her surprise, that she enjoyed the papist hymns and made friends with the nuns!

A year or so after the nuns had established themselves in Darjeeling one of the residents decided that there was need for a guide book and accordingly 'A Handbook of Darjeeling and Brief Notes' by Captain JG Hawthorn appeared. The nuns who could certainly have done with some advice must have been pleased at its publication for it is a good little book which gives all the do's and don'ts of travel by road quite explicitly.

The journey from Calcutta to Darjeeling using Dakbungalows usually occupies about seven days with baggage taking at least three weeks.

Travellers were earnestly recommended to hand their baggage over to the care of the Inland or Greenways Punchat Co. which had recently established an agency in Darjeeling. To judge by the problems travellers experienced in the journey this was good advice to be taken seriously. The charge was Rs. 5 per maund which does not seem excessive when one considers that Lloyd paid his coolies Rs. 4 for a days work.

The roads to Titalya were not good enough for horse drawn vehicles and the traveller was recommended to go by palkee or dooly dawk which should be hired.

Doolys are frequently provided without a mattress and a traveller must be prepared to take a cotton quilt or have an extra blanket to go underneath and two or three pillows and everything must be packed in a couple of ordinary tin pettarahs or baskets and these must on no account be very large or heavy.

The traveller was cautioned against arriving at a dak bungalow soaking wet and with no change of clothes and with his pettarahs some hours behind. The dak bungalows provided basic essentials of equipment and food and, continued Hawthorn, 'fresh milk is available for children early in the morning when the cows are milked before it is smoked for preserving it.' Milk was to be kept cool while travelling in a bottle wrapped in a wet jharan or cloth.

The palkees were carried at night when it was cool and the traveller was advised to prepare himself in the dak bungalow and to wear a choga or dressing gown and just go to bed in the palkee remembering to keep a blanket and umbrella with him, for however hot the night it would cool down.

As the traveller rolls into the palkee the servants at the Dakbungalow say salaams according to the liberality of the buckshees. The bearers pick up their torch and off they go to the chanting.

Hawthorn warns that the traveller is inevitably woken just as he is managing to fall asleep and usually with demands for more buksheesh. After a twelve mile stage, bearers would be changed, there were no bridges the larger rivers being crossed by raft which was, inevitably at the other side of the river with the ferryman asleep!

Joseph (later Sir Joseph) Hooker, the naturalist, friend of Darwin and explorer had much to say about the journey to Darjeeling.

At Kishangunge found that no arrangements whatever had been made for my dawk and I was fairly stranded. Luckily a thoughtful friend had provided me with letters to the scattered residents along the road and I proceeded to call on Mr. Perry, the Assistant Magistrate of the district.

A palkee having finally been arranged for him it arrived, just as he had got into bed for the night but not wanting to upset the helpful Mr. Perry he quickly moved himself into the palkee only to be woken at 4 am on 12th April:

... and found my palkee on the ground and the bearers coolly smoking their hookahs under a tree. It was raining hard, they had carried me the length of their stage, twelve miles, and there were no others to take me on. I had paid £24 for my dawk from Karagola to the hills to which I had been obliged to add a handsome douceur so I lost all patience. After entreating and waiting for several hours I found the headman of the village, and so after further disbursement I persuaded four of the six bearers to carry my empty palkee while I should walk to the next stage or until we should meet others.

At the banks of the Mahananda he again applied to the headman and had to pay the new bearers to take him to Titalya where he found no difficulty in procuring bearers to carry him the final stage. He arrived at Siliguri at 6 am on 13th April. He had not, as yet seen the mountains

so uniformly had they been shrouded by dense leaves and vapour. Here, (at Siliguri) within eight miles of their base I caught a first glimpse - not picturesque, masses clothed in forest. Siliguri stands on the edge of the Terai, the malaria belt which skirts the base of the Himalaya - every feature of geographical, botanical and zoological is new on entering this district. The change is sudden.

The Mahunuddi is a rapid river even at this season, clear and sparkling like a trout stream, it winds through a thick brushwood choked with long grasses and with a few trees chiefly of the acacia and a scarlet fruited tree. At this season only a few spring plants are in flower amongst which are sweet scented crimson asphodel and small curcuma, leaves of terrestrial orchids appeared with ferns and weeds of hot damp regions. I crossed the beds of small streams, some were dry and all were tortuous. The banks were rich and clothed with brushwood and climbers and even convolvulous vines. Intense vapour and vegetable mold - must be one of the causes of the production of malaria, the sheltered nature of the locality immediately to the base of the lofty mountains and there appeared to me to be to combine to produce stagnation and an atmosphere loaded with vapour.

He has, at this point in his journal some good word to say about the local inhabitants, the Nechi, whom he found hard working and loyal. Joseph Hooker's descriptions of forest and scenery are those of geographer and botanist, being both technical and detailed. Six miles out of Siliguri he came to a stream cutting its way through cliffs, fifteen to twenty feet high and covered with ferns, the little oxalis and other herbs. After a steep rise he arrived at the Pankhabari bungalow set in the woods on a knoll; 'as far as the eye could reach were range after range of wooded mountain, 6,000 to 8,000 feet high.'

He found that the stunted timber of the Terai had given way to a magnificent forest with deciduous trees, giant shrubs, succulents, herbs, clumps of large bamboos on the crests of hills and gullies choked with fallen vegetation, the tree trunks being covered with epiphytes and herbs.

He arrived at the Pankhabari bungalow without his luggage, nor was he able to see the bearers along the Terai road which he could see winding away below him. Fortunately it was a good bungalow and there were no particular problems.

All around the hills rise steeply, five or six thousand feet, clothed in a dense, damp, green, dripping forest. Torrents rush down the slopes their position indicated by the dipping of the forest into their beds and an occasional cloud of spray rising above a somewhat boisterous part of their course.

From the road a little above Punkabari the view is really superb... and from the hill on which I stood there ranges as far as the eye can reach, east and west, spurs stretching out onto the plains of India. These are very thickly wooded and enclose very broad, dead flat valleys apparently covered with dense forest. Secondary spurs like the one on which Punkabari is built seem to form an intermediate, neutral ground between flat and mountainous India.
Upon what a gigantic scale does the scenery here operate.

Large and troublesome ants and enormous earth worms and the noise of the great cicada so harsh and dissident. They eased as suddenly as they commenced.

The following morning my baggage arrived and leaving my palkee I mounted a pony, kindly sent to me by Mr. Hodgson, and made a very steep ascent to about 3,000 feet winding along the face of a steep, richly wooded valley. The road zig zags through innumerable lateral ravines each with its watercourse and dense jungle and leeches, the bite of these bloodsuckers gives no pain but is followed by a considerable profusion of blood.

Elephants, tigers and the occasional rhinoceros inhabit these foothills with wild boars, leopards etc but none are numerous.

1000 feet above Punkabari the vegetation was very rich and the prevalent tree is gigantic and scaled by lugumso which sometimes shin the trunks and span the forest with huge cables joining tree to tree. The trunks also clothed with parasitical orchids and still more beautifully with vines, convolvulous and begonia. The wild banana the most abundant of trees, next comes the screw pine with the straight stem and the tufted leaves eight to ten feet long waving on either side. Tree ferns, lichens and mosses at 2,000 ft.

At 4,000 ft change in vegetation, saw a very English looking bramble, raspberries, oaks, arum lilies, wild strawberries, birds were different, violets.

Hooker had left the winter of the tropics to move into the spring of the temperate zone and all the associated flowers. He stopped to rest at the Kurseong bungalow, which he found superbly placed on a narrow mountain ridge, looking down the valley of the Balasun river. He continued his journey up a very steep zig-zag up the mountain through a forest of oak, chestnut, epiphytes in vlosso, white orchids, all a mass of blossom. It was very late and dark before he arrived at the next dak bungalow, 'the nastiest looking resthouse I ever saw, stuck on a spur of the mountain, surrounded by dark forest and enveloped in mists and rains.'

It was sometime before he could rouse the dirty housekeeper who showed him into a cold room so ghostly he thought of horror stories of benighted travellers and looked at the cold sluggish beetles hanging on the damp walls. Eventually a fire began to smoke from the damp wood and later still the housekeeper produced a meal of the usual roast fowl, potatoes and custard sauce. The chicken for this meal would have been fresh killed, with boiling water poured down the dead bird's throat to speed the plucking process!

The bungalow at Panchim is at 3,000 feet and the following day brought the sight of violets, lobelias, geraniums, strawberries and honeysuckle. And so on up to cross Senchal, the view of the plains now cut off, Hooker looks down into valleys 6,000 feet deep with some spurs occupied by native clearings, a few scattered hamlets of two or three huts and the rest impenetrable dark forests. At 7,000 feet he found that chestnuts were second in abundance to the oak.

Arrived at Dorjiling on 16th April in showery cold weather. Found Mr. Charles Barnes sole tenant of the 'hotel', a round cottage type building

Kurseong Hotel showing road, railway and tea (c.1885)

22

divided up into pairs of apartments which are hired by visitors. It is usual for the Europeans to bring a full establishment of servants, bedding etc and I had not done so because I had been told that there is a furnished hotel in Dorjiling and so I was very indebted to Mr. Barnes for a kind invitation to join his mess.

Mr. Barnes was an active mountaineer and he was to accompany Hooker on several excursions to explore the mountains. Within a few days of his arrival, he went as the guest of Mr. Hodgson's up the hill at Jalapahar, now the house of the Rector of St. Paul's School, with a superb view.

The actual extent of the snowy range seen from Mr. Hodgson's windows is comprised between the arc from 8 from the north - thirty degrees to the north west or nearly a quarter of the horizon along which the perpetual snow forms an unbroken girdle or crest of frosted silver. When the mountains are covered down to 8,000 ft this white ridge stretches uninterrupted for more than 160 degrees, no known view is to be compared with this in extent, when the proximity and height of the mountains are considered for within the 8 degrees above mentioned more than 12 peaks rise above 20,000 ft and there are 9 below 15,000 ft and 7 others above 22,000. The nearest perpetual snow is on Nursing, a beautiful, sharp conical mountain, 19,130 feet high and 32 miles distant, the most remote mountain is Donkya 23,176 ft at 73 miles, while Kinchin which forms the main mass is exactly 45 miles distant.

Look again and find that the top of Kinchinjunga measuring only 4 degrees 31 feet above the level of the observer and Donkya, again which is 23,176 or about 15,700 above Mr. Hodgson's rises only 1 degree 55 above the horizon, an angle which is quite inappreciable to the eye when unaided by instruments. This view may be extended a little by ascending Senchul.

Hooker also comments on the gigantic view across the plains of India, the Teesta, Mahananda and Balasun, while nearer at hand there is gorgeous vegetation and, when Hooker was there in 1848 so much flowering magnolia that the whole hillside looked as if it had been sprinkled with snow.

The old bungalow at Tukvar Tea Estate

4

Joseph is Kidnapped

In 1848 Joseph Hooker visited Darjeeling and found that there were only about thirty European residents including some army officers, the nuns, and Hodgson who had been retired from Nepal and made his home in the 'town' because of his interest in science and exploration. There was a larger population of Asians than formerly, people from Nepal, Sikkim and Bhutan. In less than a decade the place had changed, but not as dramatically as the Calcutta newspapers had at first predicted. But the hill was no longer only the home of ghosts, the deserted village, ruined fort and monastery had changed into a small living community spied on by the Sikkim Raja but otherwise thriving.

As was mentioned earlier, one of the meanings of the Dorje of Dorje-ling, is pillar, and an early photograph of Darjeeling, before it was all built over, shows the knoll, or pillar, rising steeply on the right. A shack, the home of some Lepchas, is in the foreground and up the hillside are the stockades built to protect the town from an attack by the Sikkim Raja. The rudeness of these fortifications comes as something of a shock but it must be remembered that in the 1840s the hillmen fought with bows and arrows. For guns and ammunition they were dependent on what they could capture.

Another photograph shows a hillside covered with tree stumps and a few scattered European bungalows. The homes, spacious and comfortable-looking, are built in a style that became traditional on the tea estates. A third photograph shows the occupants preparing to go on a picnic, with a couple of ponies, a sedan chair and the ladies in crinolines, in front of one of the bungalows.

The Darjeeling Guide of 1845, three years before Hooker's visit, has much to say on the construction of the houses. The first houses were built with nothing more solid than wooden posts, and mud plaster. Hemp was added to the plaster to improve its adhesive properties. There was, of course, plenty of wood and the clay was adequate for plaster. The chimneys were generally built of brick. The roofs were of bamboo chupper (thatch), bamboo being abundant and a roof so made would last four to five years with little repair. Those who could afford it imported corrugated iron from Calcutta which was troublesome but if kept well tarred could last for 20 years!

The old bungalow at Tukvar had such an iron roof. It leaked every rains and there would be half a dozen or so large receptacles on my bedroom floor, carefully placed to catch the water and one went to sleep at night listening to the rain thundering on the roof and the drips dropping into the growing puddles in the basins. Mending leaks was always difficult because the water would often run along inside the roof till it found a suitable crack through which to drip, run, or flow into the bedroom below. The puddle usually formed at the most inconvenient places in the room causing furniture, beds and the like to be moved.

After the first few years the building of wooden houses was discontinued because the wooden posts were found to rot after just a few years. Brick and *cutcha* mortar were used. Although bricks could be made in Darjeeling, the lime, a necessary component, had to be carried up on mens' backs from Titalya, but according to the guide: 'Captain Napier has laterly experimented on lime brought from the eastern side of the Rungeet River, the result of which would have been a saving... but the Sikkim Rajah refuses to allow the removal of the lime, and we believe our Government will not take any steps to teach him better and more neighbourly courses.' Some lime deposits were later found near Kurseong.

Captain Napier of the Engineers had come to the district as a lieutenant to complete the building of the road from the plains to Darjeeling. An epic could be written on Darjeeling's link with the outside world. The building of this road was one of his first assignments and an important one in his career, helping to set the seal on his promotion up to Commander-in-Chief and Lord Napier of Magdala.

Much has been written already on the road and Thacker's 'Guide' is no exception, but unlike many, his has an optimistic tone. The 'Guide' considered that the line had been judiciously selected and the construction was as stable and permanent as the soil and materials at hand would permit:

The whole road is superficially dressed and bound at the outer edge
with a binding of timber fastened by stakes, driven 3 feet into the
ground and 3 feet apart, or supported on a revetment of dry stone
masonry.

·   In Darjeeling itself, the Chowrasta near Observatory Hill, the site of the ruined monastery was made the focal point of the town. It was from here that the town's roads radiated out in all directions, and in later years the fashionable sat or strolled and listened to the band playing as they watched the sun setting over the eternal snows. Later it was here I saw the old and weary sit as the red of the sunset gave way to the grey of night. They sat in silence, remembering bygone days.

But in 1848, when Hooker arrived, there were only a few buildings and none of Calcutta's fashionable. The only public building was the Superintendent's cutchery, combining his office with his house. On Darjeeling Hill stood a neat wattle and daub bungalow with an iron roof, St. Andrew's Church, and a small fort or neat stockade. The 'old' hotel had 28 apartments and there was also the 'new' hotel. There were also, scattered about, some 30 private houses which had, for the most part, been built of wattle and daub and had roofs of bamboo since most could not afford the iron roofs. Darjeeling existed but was a far cry from being the great sanatorium Calcutta so badly needed.

St. Andrew's Church highlights the building problems. Built of poor quality bricks, made locally, the church was always damp and though used, it was never consecrated. It looked fine, a neat British church, a landmark on the hillside and one which often shows up in the old photographs. It was to have a short life.

To administer this new district, the East India Company appointed a Dr. Archibald Campbell, the Resident at Kathmandu. He was 27 when he first came to India, Kathmandu being his first appointment. He was in Khatmandu for several years and had the opportunity not only of making a lasting friend of Bahadur Singh, the Nepalese ruler, but to learn to understand and have sympathy with the ordinary Nepalese people. In 1839 he was a member of the commission to settle the boundary dispute between Sikkim and Nepal and in July of the same year, when 34 years of age, he was appointed to take charge of the hill station, Darjeeling which, according to the records, then consisted of not more than twenty families and some hillmen who had settled.

The wooden house which Archibald Campbell established himself in near to the centre of the town was small and served as home and office. A spark from the fire set the place ablaze in 1840 and the doctor lost not only the official records but, more devastating for him, his research notes.

His new home was ready the following year, when he imported a housekeeper, in the form of his young bride, Emily Ann Lamb, a ward of court. She was transported to Darjeeling along with some valuable tea seeds to plant in his garden. His home had a magnificent view and his wife was to flourish and prove most fertile, but the site was too cold for tea and his personal experiments in tea growing were not at first successful and his seed was wasted. Tea companies were now being formed in Assam where some men like Roberts and the Williamson family had gone past the first experimental stages of growing tea and were now sending boxes regularly to market. As others followed their example so the demand for tea seed grew, with most supplies still coming from China.

However, as tea seed was also distributed to others in Darjeeling who were prepared to experiment, it was not long before there was some success. In 1852 Mr. Jackson noted that both Assam and China bushes were now doing well in Campbell's garden as well as in the more extensive plantations of Dr. Withecombe, the Civil Surgeon and Major Crommelin of the Engineers at the lower elevation of Lebong. Although there were some, including Dr. Hooker who considered that Darjeeling had too much moisture and too little sun for tea, experiments continued and by 1856 they were moving into the commercial stage. It was in 1857 that the Rev. T Boaz reported that tea had been raised from seed at a place he called 'Takvar' by Captain Masson, at Kurseong by Mr. Smith and Mr. Martin on the Kurseong flats, and between Kurseong and Pankhabari by Captain Samler, agent of the Darjeeling Tea Company. In fact, no sooner had tea been proved to be viable than companies were formed for its development - the Kurseong and Darjeeling Tea Company, the Land Mortgage Company, The Darjeeling Tea Concern. By 1864 there were 34 tea gardens and by the end of 1866 there were 39 gardens with 10,000 acres under cultivation and an annual production of 43,000 pounds of tea.

To promote tea in Darjeeling was not all Dr. Campbell's work or achievements. 1842 was a busy year for him, it began with the first of 'new' Darjeeling's earthquakes, just a minor shock, nothing to alarm the inhabitants unduly. In March the notes he had submitted on the Sepehas and other tribes were declared to be 'interesting and of value', in July his first child, Helen Maria, was born and just twelve days later, leaving his young wife, he was off to Bhutan on a mission.

The development of trade was important and to this end trading marts, like the one at Titalya were set up. Over one hundred years later I went to one of these marts or melas, at Pedong, on the border with Sikkim and the route down to the Rishi and up to the Nathu La pass into Tibet. It could not have changed much in all those years. The mart had been strategically placed to cater for the small farmers and traders as well as the merchants. Photographs of this mart show the small, ordinary hillmen and fashionable wealthy Tibetans, their womenfolk standing erect and proud in their gay aprons and wearing tall hats trimmed with fur although at 2,500 feet this was hardly necessary but added the appearance of fashion and occasion.

To further the progress of trade, roads were needed and Campbell supplemented Napier's main road from the plains and those in the township itself with a network of district roads built by the Sebundy Corps of Sappers and Miners who had the dual function of being road builders and the main force on which Darjeeling depended for its security from the Sikkim Raja and the Bhutanese. Again the word 'road' is used in a descriptive sense of the routes up and down the mountainside by which one travelled, such as the 'road' to Tukvar. A century later this 'road' was much as it had been, just widened here and there to allow a car access. Of this road the Bishop of Barrackpore was to write, "Lovely" is not, however, exactly the adjective one would use to describe the road which leads down to Tukvar from the main road, though the scenery is all that could be desired. The road twists and turns, with a corner every fifty or hundred yards, corkscrewing its way down the mountainside, dropping 2000 feet in two and a half miles. Only a powerful small car, like an Austin A40 [this was written in 1954] or a jeep or Land Rover, can negotiate it, and it is definitely not a road for nervous drivers or passengers.' These 'roads' were necessary and functional, no more.

In 1844, the year Campbell graduated from being an 'Assistant Surgeon' to a 'Surgeon' the site for the first troop cantonment was chosen at Katapahar by

28

Senchal. One can only speculate that the day of the decision was a particularly fine hot one. This impractical site was doomed to disaster right from the start. It was too high, too cold, and too mist ridden and had to be abandoned in 1867 for Jalapahar. One particularly miserable, foggy day a company of men lashed themselves to a gun and in a gruesome mass suicide were hurtled to their death over Ghoom rocks. When I revisited Senchal it was impossible not to be struck by the gloom of January's cold. Cloud hung suspended, motionless while tiny droplets of water congregated on the lichens and mosses which, like cold and dusty cobwebs, festooned the cryptamaria pines. The silence was complete, no insect, no bird, no distant hum of urban life. It even felt too gloomy for the ghosts and yet, where the forest had been cleared one could see the remains of the old cantonments and the moss covered greens of the golf course, built in optimistic days.

By the time that Dr. Hooker reached Darjeeling the five Loreto nuns were well established in their 'convent' and a few more buildings had gone up but the town, though well known, was still not flourishing. It was not only the Nepalese who were sitting on the fence and waiting.

Dr. Hooker was a young man who had already made a name for himself as explorer and naturalist. He came to Darjeeling on the advice of Lord Auckland, the Governor General and of Dr. Falkland. Each, independent of the other, recommended Sikkim as 'being ground untrodden by traveller or naturalist.' He was also given a grant of £400 to assist his work.

On his arrival in Darjeeling Dr. Hooker called on the Superintendent, Dr. Campbell, not only as a courtesy call but for advice and assistance in his work of collecting botanical specimens and in his explorations. As he planned to work in Sikkim he needed an introduction to the Raja. Because of the Treaty of Titalya the British, that is the East India Company, regarded the Raja as a dependent. It was assumed, by those living in the comfort and heat of Calcutta that the Raja would be willing, nay glad to assist the British explorer.

Lord Auckland, or his advisors, had overlooked one important fact - the Sikkim Raja, like most of the ruling class, was a Tibetan and a vassal of a country which had closed its borders to the west. Everything about the Raja was Tibet orientated, not only did he have a Tibetan wife but actually preferred to live in Tibet, finding the climate of the Chumbi valley more to his taste than that of Sikkim, which was wet. And as Darjeeling became more and more established and the opportunities of trade developed, so did his regret at the gift of the land.

Hooker's first job was to make a detailed examination of British Sikkim, paying attention to the plants, walking sometimes in the company of Mr. Barnes, the mountaineer who had befriended him on his arrival. It was nearly a year after his arrival in Darjeeling that Hooker crossed into Sikkim with plans to go as far as Tibet itself. He ran into all kinds of problems with those in Sikkim whom he had relied on to help him. In spite of this he did reach the Jelep La Pass and was able to have a good view of his special mountain Chumolhari which was across the border in Tibet. Difficulties with the Sikkimese continued to such an extent that Dr. Campbell thought it advisable to join him in November 1849 in spite of the fact that his young wife was again heavily pregnant. Both the Dewan and the Raja of Sikkim were in Tibet at the time, but Campbell, like everyone else, misjudged them.

The right hand man of the Sikkim Raja was the Dewan Namguay who saw Darjeeling as encroaching on his trading rights as well as being a source of irritation over slaves, resulting in frequent kidnappings and demands that slaves be returned. When the Dewan heard that Campbell had joined Hooker on Sikkim's soil, he could not resist the opportunity of ordering them to be kidnapped, or taken prisoner.

From his home in Tibet, the Dewan considered the kidnapping of Campbell as a solution to all his problems. Nothing, however was to happen. Although Darjeeling was told that the two doctors had been captured there was no reply, no action, nothing. Those in Calcutta and particularly those in Darjeeling appeared to be unconcerned that the two eminent men had been taken hostage. It was confusing for the Dewan and the Raja.

The answer was very simple. The letters to Darjeeling from Sikkim contained various matters and only included a line stating that Campbell was detained at Tunglung till a favourable answer should be received. Because the letter was written in Tibetan only the interpreter could read it and since the correspondence appeared to contain matters which only Archibald Campbell could deal with, the interpreter put it aside, not reading right through to the end, and in particular, the last line containing the information most relevant to the prisoners - namely their capture. Thus it was that news of capture and imprisonment remained unknown for weeks. Meanwhile Campbell was not allowed to write and the replies to letters he had received before his capture were seized and burnt.

Sikkim threatened to attack Darjeeling. The residents who had overlooked the fact that Sikkim had no army and few muskets to speak of, took the threat seriously. They were also alarmed, as the Dewan hoped they would be, by the information that the Tibetans had gathered a great army and were marching to support Sikkim.

While all this was happening the nuns went about their business as usual, they were not going to panic, there was no need, Mother Superior recognised the Lepchas, who would make the bulk of the Sikkim attack, for the cowards they were, and considered Tibet far too far into the mountains to have any interest in Darjeeling.

Meanwhile Campbell and Hooker, imprisoned in Sikkim, had the frustration of witnessing the great delight and amusement of their captors when they heard of the panic which their threatened attack had created in Darjeeling. They relished the fact that not only had the guards been called in from all the outposts, but the ladies were huddled into one house while the men prepared to fight to the death.

On 15th November the prisoners' spirits were raised by the news that the Dewan was on his way from Tibet, because Campbell had, in the past, considered him sensible. They were to be disappointed. The Dewan arrived with a large train which included lamas and women riding side saddle. It was an impressive train. The Dewan himself wore a large, black-brimmed hat, decorated with butterflies and tassels, while one of his train sported a Chinese hat. No doubt this hat was intended to impress not only the prisoners, but the local lamas and khasyas who did not approve of what had happened. The whole party was preceded by some sepoys with matchlocks.

Campbell was to be disappointed, the arrival of the Dewan changed nothing. It was a bizarre situation, the local khasyas, lamas and other noblemen disapproved of the proceedings and even felt able to send presents to the prisoners, and yet were unable to have any influence on their release, although they did refuse to attend the council.

Weary of their captivity, Hooker kept up his meteorological register and in his journal refers to Campbell's cheerfulness in spite of his private concern for his young wife.

The Dewan did nothing to improve the conditions under which they were held except to reduce the guard because of the shortage of food. In fact the prisoners were, at one point, paying for the guards' food to be supplemented out of their own pockets. During all of this the group, including the prisoners, moved slowly towards the frontier with Darjeeling.

Hooker records that each morning they would awake to the echo of many conch trumpets and cymbals from the valley temples and after dark they sat over a fire with a small, very dirty, Lepcha child for company who as well as having much curiosity was able to get a Tibetan jews harp which helped to improve their evening's entertainment. She was a great mimic, this child and enjoyed their music.

There was a sad incident when one of their servants returned from Darjeeling so frightened that no amount of kindness, nothing could persuade him to speak intelligibly.

Hooker's journal was becoming less cheerful. They wondered whether the man had been beaten or threatened or was very concerned for their fate. They knew that the man, Toba Singh, had coolly suggested to the 'amban' (emissary) that he 'despatch' Campbell as being the best possible solution to the current deadlock. Both Campbell and Hooker were ignorant of any plans being made in Darjeeling and they were sure that some steps would be taken to effect their release. In the meantime they continued to worry that they would end their days in the Teesta river.

They were guarded by one sepoy with a knife and Toba Singh, whom Hooker described as being a dirty, cross-eyed fellow and a barefaced liar. He was also cringeing and obsequious. Apart from Chebu Lama he was the only Bhutia around who could speak Hindi.

They moved on slowly towards Darjeeling and there were days when the Dewan appeared to treat them with civility. On one occasion he even invited them to dinner but then gave them putrid fish to eat. This, however, was followed by a gift of the best tobacco to smoke and an insistence that they eat indigestion pills which persuaded Hooker that he was being poisoned. The Dewan even sat beside them, putting his arms round their shoulders in a too friendly gesture.

Each day they came a little nearer to Darjeeling as if there was a magnet in the place. The nearer they got, the more frightened the Dewan became. He dillied and dallied, dressed up in his fine regalia of saffron silk robes, perhaps to impress himself more than his fellow countrymen and the prisoners.

Campbell, worrying about his young wife and the baby, was not as well as Hooker as the days went by. They were both at the whim and fancy of the Dewan's moods. No negotiation was possible and could not be possible with the outside world not knowing what was happening. Days passed in deadlock.

One morning, when it was almost Christmas and they were not too far from the Teesta and the crossing into British Sikkim, Hooker decided that it was time to act. Pulling himself up to his full height, standing on his British dignity, he explained to the Dewan that the British had only one special day in the year, Christmas Day, while the Sikkimese had many. It was important for the Dewan's safety that they be home for Christmas.

Impressed, the Dewan let them go. They crossed the Teesta and rode up the Takdah ridge to be home for Christmas Eve and Archibald Campbell was able to greet his baby daughter, Josephine, born on 27th November.

F.L.B.
PRAYER WHEEL.

5

I Did Call For A Cup Of Tea

Imagine a giant walking up the side of a steep mountain. As he leaves the steamy valley by Singla the impression left by his step is light. He grows weary and when he reaches Tukvar the tread is heavier, the impression more marked; he makes a good step at North Point but at Darjeeling he pauses, resting on both feet before carrying on with shorter strides to Jalapahar, Katapahar, Senchal and finally the summit at Tiger Hill. Where once that giant put his feet, man was able to build his hamlets, villages or, where the space allowed, Darjeeling.

At the bottom of one of the spurs branching out from Darjeeling is the great Rangit river, a bridging point into Sikkim. Climbing up the ridge, are first the bungalows of Singla tea estate, then Barnsbeg, the Tukvar, North Point and Darjeeling. The giant had paused a moment at Tukvar, enjoying the cooler air and the view of the snowy mountains and the footprint he left on the hillside was, the Lepchas thought, shaped liked a fishhook - Tak Var.

Ignorant of the harsh realities of these gigantic mountains with their enormous weather systems, a band of Moravians sought to establish a mission settlement at Tukvar where the climate, while cool, was warmer than Darjeeling and the view superb. Some of the forest had already been cleared by the Lepchas. There was a small bustee - or hamlet - close by. They cleared more forest and built a very strong and sturdy church, established a farm and began their new life. They had been encouraged by the Rev. Start to build a totally self sufficient mission. They did not stay long enough to give the experiment a fair chance or to make their work a reality. Mr. Treutler abandoned his farm at Tukvar to make one at North Point, closer to the expanding markets. Muhler, who became friendly with Hooker and helped him with his weather observations, also found living in Darjeeling more congenial. Even the dedicated Karl Niebel moved his wife and large family up to Darjeeling close to the Campbell family where they lived in the tiniest European house in the town. From the security of Darjeeling Niebel carried on with his work translating the Gospel into the Lepcha language and ministering to the hillmen.

Hope Town was another project to fail. A 'good life' was planned by some idealists who sought to create their own peaceful society. They wished to develop a community of smallholders and some of their dreams smacked of the spirit of the Pilgrim Fathers. But the harsh environment is no friend to idealists or dreamers. Those who did not sell out to the expanding tea industry joined it, and like Mr. Martin found it a profitable business.

33

By the time that Captain Hawthorn wrote his Darjeeling Guide, the hillsides had changed. As the Captain wrote:

Nine years ago on the occasion of our first visit to Darjeeling, with the exception of the station of Darjeeling itself and a few native clearings scattered here and there on the hill sides, these mountains as far as the eye could reach were covered with primeval forest, the magnificent luxuriance of whose foliage was indescribably splendid; but now, alas, for the scenery, though perhaps the better for the country, fire and axe have swept away the majestic tree and flowery creeper to make way for plantations of that little bush from whose leaves are prepared the beverage that "cheers but not inebriates".

Darjeeling was one of the last areas in India to plant out tea and therefore was able to avoid some of the worst effect of tea-mania with its subsequent crash. By the time the Darjeeling estates were opening up some of the early mistakes of the first tea planters had been corrected.

For a contemporary picture of the scene in Darjeeling we turn to a letter in the *Friend of India* 2nd January, 1862.

...before 1855 there were probably no more than 1,000 plants on the station - it was merely known that the tea tree would grow there.

In 1855 4 or 5 acres of ground were sown by a private individual with tea seed.

In 1856 the first tea company was formed under the management of an invalid officer.

In 1857 the second tea company was formed.

In 1859 two more companies were started.

In 1860 and '61 more progress has been made and at present there are about twenty five plantations, large and small, established from 3 - 4,000 acres each and already planted out.

Tea Planting in Darjeeling is not a mere 'experiment or an amusement of gentlemen fond of a quiet life'. It is true one or two military officers conducted the first experiments, but at present time but two officers continue to be engaged in the occupation, all the rest of the planters are of the same class as have settled in Assam and Cachar and it is a serious enterprise, i.e. is being conducted with as much energy and determination as characterises the operations in these eastern districts.

There are no 'drawbacks' greater than are found in Assam and Cachar.

Labour is abundant and the communications are being improved. One or two mistakes upon a small scale were made at the commencement in planting at too high an elevation, but the plantations generally are on the low elevations and in the valleys where the plant grows rapidly and yields leaf abundantly.

It had been discovered that the Chinese variety of tea suited the slower growth of the Darjeeling climate better than the vigorous Assam varieties. And, of course, it was soon discovered that Darjeeling could produce a champagne among teas.

From the very beginning when Grant was trying to persuade the East India Company to establish Darjeeling, he made the point that there would be no problem with labour. This was to be the case. In the neighbouring state of Nepal there were large numbers of people with no land and no work who were happy to man the new tea-estates. It therefore comes as no surprise to note that the 1931 census recorded 92,970 as having Nepali as their mother tongue while 37,444 spoke Bengali and 22,595 Hindi.

It is one of those ironical quirks of history that the British defeated the Nepalese and expelled them from Sikkim only to encourage their return to man the tea estates. This large number of Nepalis not surprisingly has led to the formation of the Gurkha league and to some of the present political problems.

6

Peak XV - Where No Bird Can Fly

Because many of the tourists who flock to Darjeeling today include a visit to Tiger Hill to see the sun rise over Mount Everest, the highest mountain in the world, it is felt necessary to write a few words about this mountain.

Kanchenjunga so dominates at Darjeeling that the early surveyors, explorers and visitors quite reasonably assumed that it must be the highest mountain in the world. Kanchenjunga was surveyed along with the other peaks but some of them remained as dots on a map with just numbers to them. When Hooker was in Darjeeling in 1848 - 1850 he referred to Mount Kanchenjunga as being the highest mountain in the world, though he does make reference to the impressive group of mountains which were up to one hundred miles distant which could be as high. The actual 'discovery' of Mount Everest is something of an anti-climax except for the 'Computer' concerned. The mountain is recorded as having been surveyed in 1841, but the data, along with that of many other mountains, had to wait to be calculated. Kanchenjunga, in the meantime, reigned supreme in men's minds.

In his book, 'Kingdom of Adventure, Everest' James Ramsey Ullman describes the 'discovery' of this giant of mountains:

The first scene in the series of dramas which together constitute the story of Everest, has for its setting prosaic Indian Government offices where one day in 1852 the Bengali Chief Computer rushed into the room of the Surveyor-General, Sir Andrew Waugh, breathlessly saying, "Sir, I have discovered the highest mountain in the world!"

The office of the Trigonometrical Survey had been long engaged on a series of observations of the peaks of Nepal from the plains of India. Native names had been officially adopted where they were known, but many of these mountains, so numerous, massed together and towering one above the other, were nameless even to local people. Numbers therefore had to be given to distinguish them. Among these unnamed peaks was one 'Peak XV'. Observations of it were recorded but were not worked out for some years afterwards.

Then, leisurely working over the accumulated data, the Computer made his dramatic discovery and immediately hastened to his chief with the news.

Excited as he was, he could have had no conception of the adventures to which his mathematical calculations were destined to lure men. The sequel was to be a struggle with gods and demons - existing only in the minds of the dwellers in the remote country of the mountain, but none the less real opponents. It was to be a contest with nature in her cruellest moods, waged where the earth, surging upwards, thrusts herself - stark, bleak and lonely - through her enveloping atmosphere in the Great Void.

Immediately the officials got busy. Carefully the observations from all six stations, whence this Peak XV had been observed, were checked, and the mean height of 29,002 feet was arrived at. The measurement was in later years carefully rechecked and raised to 29,145 feet. Sir Andrew Waugh named the mountain after Sir George Everest, his predecessor, the Surveyor-General of India, under whose directions the triangulations had been started, but afterwards the Everest expeditions discovered the Tibetan name is Chomo Lungma, which means "Goddess Mother of the World".

All sorts of people have from time to time told stories of mountains higher than Everest; but it is definitely known that there is no higher mountain, and it became the dream and goal of explorers and mountaineers.

But nobody could reach it, although it was so tantalisingly near. It was computed to be only one hundred and ten miles, as the crow flies, from Darjeeling...

After the 1880s and again at the turn of the century more observations were taken of Everest from places near Darjeeling which included Sandakphu and Tiger Hill so that they were measuring a mountain 87 to 107 miles away as the crow flies.

The mountain, Everest or Peak XV was so remote that no one except the few who lived on or near its slopes knew of its existence which makes the memories of Tenzing all the more valuable.

Tenzing Norkay, the first man, along with Edmund Hillary to stand on the summit of Everest has this to say of the mountain under which he was born.

Many times as a child I saw it, of course, rising high in the sky to the north above the tops of the nearer mountains. But it was not Everest then. It was Chomolungma. Usually Chomolungma is said to mean "Goddess Mother of the World ". Sometimes "Goddess Mother of the Wind." But it did not mean either of these when I was a boy in Solo Khumbu. Then it meant "The Mountain So High No Bird Can Fly Over It." That is what all Sherpa mothers used to tell their children, what my own mother told me and it is the name I still like best for this mountain that I love.

Although Mount Everest, as seen from Darjeeling's Tiger Hill looks small and dignified, it never fails to impress in these mountains which are surely home to giants. For those who have both the time and energy the view is better still from Tonglu or along the Singalela ridge to Sandakphu. Hooker visited this ridge in 1848 with his friend Barnes from the hotel. Over a hundred years later it formed the first few days' marching for the successful expedition to climb Kanchenjunga. It was from these sites that many of the surveys were undertaken.

Tonglu and Sandakphu was one of the set 'treks' one could make from Darjeeling and the nearest an ordinary Englishwoman like me could, in 1955, get to feeling that she was walking on the roof of the world. On the one side the walker looks across a deep valley of the little Rangit and the Rungpo to Darjeeling and on the other the walker looks over into Nepal and up to the great mountain peaks. The trek, for which special permits had to be obtained, took me and my party ten days in November 1954. We began, as had the Kanchenjunga Expedition, by walking along the border of Nepal and Sikkim, along the Singalela range. Staying at Dak bungalows we were able to watch the sun both rising and setting over this giantland, over both the Kanchenjunga range, the Everest group and all the lower fantasia. And, because we were higher, by some three thousand feet, than Tiger Hill the view was 3,000 feet better. Better still to have gone higher but in 1954 the high treks were no longer possible because of border troubles.

Treks were much encouraged and references and guidebooks go back to the 1880s. Although we had Sherpa porters to carry our gear, our party was too poor to hire ponies as many did. And, before the border troubles put an end to tourists going higher than 12,000 feet those wishing to go higher rode on yaks.

However, walking in the Sikkim hills is a bit more than an after dinner stroll and not to be recommended unless one is reasonably fit to start with. Knees not used to walking down hill can suffer most terribly and mountain sickness can hardly be recommended as a cure!

The excitement of Everest is in the adventure and the challenge of the mountain. It has the power of a magnet to draw one up into the mountains, to get higher and higher. It is not for these pages to discuss the work of Everest exploration, nor that of the Indian explorers such as Hari Ram Ganderson Singh who went disguised into the area but Darjeeling has been a centre for mountaineering and some mention must be made of the sport.

New ground in mapping these mountains was made when in 1933 the Houston Mount Everest Expedition set out, not just to fly over Mount Everest and Kanchenjunga but to take aerial survey photographs. These filled some of the gaps on the world's maps. Their flight, so quickly over, tends to be overlooked by the struggle to climb the mountain but its achievement was, in its time, considerable. It was in the days when aviators were breaking records, reaching new heights and competition was strong. Britain took the prize of being the first to fly over the summit of Everest.

In these days of sophisticated photography the thought of a man standing up to take photographs out of the top of a plane flying over Everest is in the regions of fantasy. The expedition flew Westlands which to the modern jet age were mere small box-like planes, so 'simple' that the photographer could lie on the floor, the hatch open and look down into the mountains. He could also stand up with his head out of the cockpit for unrestricted views over the huge Mount Everest. The cameras used were heavy, less sophisticated and allergic to the cold.

To help keep the links with the past, with the observing, computing and map making of the Himalayas one of the observers in the expedition was LVS Blacker, a descendent of Colonel Valentine Blacker, the Surveyor-General of India from 1823 to 1826 and the man responsible for the completion of the first map of Hindustan. His pupil, or disciple, was George Everest.

The expedition was based at Purnea which is about eighty miles from Siliguri at the foot of the hills. (It was from Purnea that the Loreto nuns obtained flour for their daily bread in the early days before the Darjeeling administration had organised the grocery supplies.) Using weather reports from various weather stations at and around Darjeeling, the groundwork and preparations for the flights were carefully made. Dr. Graham of the Kalimpong Homes made contact with the expedition who even agreed to drop leaflets over the town of Kalimpong on one of their flights over Kanchenjunga.

By today's standards their equipment was primitive and their sturdy Westlands even more so. Caught in a down draught as they were approaching Everest's peak they lost 2,000 feet but, fortunately, were able to pull back up to clear the summit. The cameraman, the chief observer in the plane, Blacker, tells his story:

> Now, without getting up from a prone position, I could move myself back a little on my elbows, open the hatchway in the floor, and look vertically down on the amazing mountainscape, bare of trees, seamed with great glaciers, and interspersed with streaks of scree and shale. This was the beginning of the range, insignificant enough to our eyes at the height we were, which rises up to the culminating 24,000 feet peak of Chamlang. Then shutting the hatchway and, laboriously taking great care to keep the oxygen pipe unentangled, and myself clear of all the various electrical wires, I could stand up and look again through the top of the cockpit. I caught a glimpse over the pilot's shoulder of the brilliant red light on his dashboard, which flashed for a moment as the camera shutter operated itself.
>
> Up went our machine into a sky of indescribable blue, until we came to a level with the great culminating peak itself.
> Then, to my astonished eyes, northwards over the shoulder of the mountain, across the vast bare plateau of Tibet, a group of snow-clad peaks uplifted itself. I hesitated to conjecture the distance at which they lay in the heart of that almost trackless country, for by some trick of vision the summits seemed even higher than that of Mount Everest.

The astonishing picture of this great mountain itself, whose plume for a moment seemed to diminish in length, and with its tremendous sullen cliffs, set off the whiteness of Makalu, was a sight which must for ever remain in one's mind.

...So I went on, now exposing plates, now lifting the heavy cinema camera to run off fifty feet or so of film. I crouched down again, struggling to open the hatchway, to take a photograph through the floor. Everything by now, all the metal parts of the machine, was chilled with cold, the cold of almost interstellar space. The fastenings were stiff and the metal slides had almost seized. I struggled with them, the effort making me pant for breath, and I squeezed my mask on to my face to get all the oxygen possible. I had to pause and, suddenly, with the door half-open I became aware, almost perceptibly, of a sensation of dropping through space... We had suddenly lost two thousand feet in this great down-draught of the winds, and it seemed as though we should never clear the crags of the South Peak on the way to Everest now towering in front of us. However, the alarm was short-lived, for our splendid engine took us up through the great overfall. Again we climbed; slowly, yet too quickly for one who wants to make use of every moment, our aeroplane came to the curved chisel-like summit of Everest, crossing it, so it seemed to me, just a hair's breadth over its menacing summit. The crest came up to meet me as I crouched peering through the floor, and I almost wondered whether the tail skid would strike the summit. I laboured incessantly, panting again for breath to expose plates and films, each lift of the camera being a real exertion. Every now and then my eyes swam a little and I looked at the oxygen flow-meter to find it reading its maximum...
Now I had worked my way up again to a standing position, with the cockpit roof fully open and its flaps fastened back. I had my head and shoulders out into the slip stream which had become strangely bereft of its accustomed force. I was astonished for a moment till I suddenly remembered that the wind here only weighed a quarter as much as at sea-level. Now I could take photographs over the top of the machine...
Thus almost, and indeed before I expected it we swooped over the summit and a savage period of toil began. The pilot swung the machine skilfully again towards the westward into the huge wind force sweeping downwards over the crest.

Before they finally packed their bags to leave India, Blacker, Fellowes and Etherton went up to Darjeeling with the film party. They drove up the hill, following, as everyone does the line of the railway, Etherton gives us a breathtaking description of this journey up the foothills of the mountain they had recently flown over.

We came part of the way by this toy line, a fascinating experience through a wealth of plants, of bamboo and tea gardens. It is a world of its own; the sort of world one has conjured up in books, a world that is expressed in vegetation, and always when going up to Darjeeling, you mount higher and higher, passing round curves so that you can almost touch the carriages running parallel to your own. It goes on over slopes that look as though they might topple down at any moment from the vibration of the train; then it passes over a bridge spanning a mountain torrent above the place it passed five minutes ago and below another which it will pass in five minutes' time.

Twisting and turning, the little railway carries you up into the clouds and Darjeeling. It is perched on a long ridge with other ridges round it.

General view of Darjeeling (1871)

41

7

Give Me Rum Not Beer

In the winter of 1859 a demonstration of force followed the kidnapping of the two doctors, Campbell and Hooker. The East India Company annexed 640 square miles of the Terai, invaded Sikkim for a few weeks and stopped paying the Raja Rs. 6,000 per annum which had been a 'voluntary' contribution on the part of the Company in recognition of the Raja's kind gift of Darjeeling and for his lost revenues. This was not sufficient, however, to impress upon the Sikkim authorities that the British did not like to be trifled with. Negotiation was not part of the Sikkim life style, not something they understood. They understood force, kidnappings, threats and cowards.

The situation deteriorated. Nothing was done and the rulers in Sikkim assumed a stance of power which resulted in numerous kidnappings of British subjects. The Sikkim authorities considered their actions to be justified on the grounds that the people kidnapped had been slaves. Then, by kidnapping a young girl, the Dewan touched the honour of the Darjeeling men and challenged their chivalry.

There had to be action; the desk wallahs in Calcutta turned to the professional soldiers for advice and to none other than the Commander-in-Chief, Sir Charles Napier. He was the man, it must be remembered, who as a lieutenant had so impressed the world when he took over and completed building the road to Darjeeling after the first engineer had found the job almost too much and was so frequently ill. Napier knew the country and being an experienced soldier as well as an engineer his opinions were eagerly sought. He was quick to advise against any kind of military action because Sikkim was unsuitable for British troops. He then went on to become the hero of Magdala and win a peerage.

The decision to take no action did nothing to help those living in Darjeeling and no-one wished the Raja's takeover bid to succeed. The dedicated, if not a trifle foolhardy, Campbell led the Sabundy Sappers where no trained army wished to tread. The brave band of road builders and Darjeeling peacekeepers marched to Rinchenpong.

On their way they were given every possible assistance by the local Sikkimese and Chebu Lama who saw a much better future for them under the British and, no doubt, who also assumed that the British power would defeat the Raja.

There are two versions of what happened next. One, possibly the official one, suggested that Campbell had been attacked by 300 Sikkimese for fourteen hours and had fought against 800 men in an open stockade, killing 40 and losing only one killed and nine wounded.

The other version suggests that when rumours of a vast army of Tibetans, Bhutias and some Sikkimese reached their ears, the locals took fright and warned Campbell, and more particularly his brave army of Sappers, of the impending attack. It is unlikely that Campbell was unduly worried by the rumours but they spread panic amongst his little band. The Sabundy Sappers deserted the big gun and, even worse, its ammunition. They even threw away their rifles so that, passing as coolies, they could make good their escape back to Darjeeling.

The outcome vindicated Napier, but the problem remained. Life in Darjeeling was threatened. If Sikkim was invincible, Darjeeling was doomed. Was the British army really afraid to face an enemy armed with poisoned bows and arrows and a few captured guns they did not know how to use? Was the jungle really so impenetrable? The residents in Darjeeling were very anxious. The enemy was patrolling their territory and even threatening their communications with Pankhabari. Fortunately there were some in Calcutta who realised that action had to be taken. It was suggested that Sir Charles was getting on, and his advice was touched with age and weariness.

On 12th December 1860, Colonel Gwaler, an officer experienced in fighting in impossible terrain, was commissioned 'to give the enemy his first lesson.' The order, received by telegram, told him to take command of the expedition to Sikkim. Ordered to go with him as the Political Officer was the 30 year old Ashley Eden, third son of the third Lord Auckland, Bishop of Bath and Wells. It was to him that Gwaler had to refer all his plans and problems.

Before the Colonel began to organise the campaign he organised himself. He went first to Calcutta to lay his dak and organise his palkee bearers, arrange for troops and stores and to buy a copy of Hooker's Journal which he read on the road. Taking with him a pack saddle, two leather portmanteaux, a blanket and a piece of tarpaulin, he took the train to the Ganges, which he crossed by steamer. From the Ganges he had the inevitable palkee ride to Pankhabari. Then followed the steep climb up the mountainside to Kurseong, a journey which appalled him; it was up this comparatively narrow track, already littered with tea chests and stores for Darjeeling, that his army, his supplies, everything for the success of his venture had to be carried, and quickly at that. From Kurseong he was relieved to find that there were 36 miles of good narrow road, 'I think the width was twelve feet', to Darjeeling.

In Darjeeling he bought the best pony he could find and a second one. He had two cane baskets made to fit his pack saddle, which he considered to be stiff, good and better able to keep their shape yet still be more yielding than boxes, which were liable to be broken or ripped. He paused to see the snowy peaks which he described as 'magnificent mass, seemed to be in two miles of me not 40. I could not but be impressed.' The valleys were deep dug and the torrents raging.

At this stage in proceedings Gwaler considered himself lucky, when referring to Hooker's Journal, he says 'never was officer commanding a force favoured with fuller or more lucid work on country'. He had also read the Military Report of 1st January 1850 written after Campbell and Hooker had been kidnapped and there had been a punitive venture across the Teesta and into the 'plains' of Sikkim. This report was all pessimism. There was nothing but impenetrable jungle of brushwood and briars. The trees were huge and often felled across the path so that soldiers were impeded without even firing a shot. There were rumours of booby traps to undermine the morale of troops who had to cope with a 'savage or an uncivilised' enemy. The Tibetan fighters had a fearful reputation.

The Raja who was not only Tibetan himself, also received a stipend from Tibet, his wife, the Dewan and most of those in authority were all Tibetan. It was an awesome foe Gwaler faced.

The back-up given to the expedition also proved Napier right. The British army was not sufficiently organised to provision and mount a campaign in the Sikkim hills. The problem of transporting equipment from Calcutta to Titalya and Pankhabari at the foot of the hills was so tremendous that horses died of overwork. The position was exacerbated by the transportation of unsuitable provisions at the expense of the necessities, and the gallons of beer which should never have been transported to Titalya on the overworked horses, had to be abandoned to ferment in the sun, so that the real necessities of war could be taken into the hills. Rum was of paramount importance. The Sikhs ate atta; no atta was available but they would fight on a diet of rice and corn if they had rum as a digestive. And then the roughness of the hill tracks had been underestimated and since there were no cobblers, the one pair of boots per man was worn out half way to Darjeeling and long before the soldiers had caught a glimpse of the enemy let alone the frontier.

It may have been the first time, but it was not the last, that the British army found itself in Darjeeling with equipment suitable only for the tropics!

Gwaler continued to be worried about the lack of atta 'therefore we must have rum as rice and butta (indian corn) alone make them sick.' He was anxious about transport since he doubted the coolies; he had to use coolies recruited in Darjeeling as he dared not rely on the local force.

He wrote of the problems of transport. Troops and stores were converging on Pankhabari on two good roads, but there was only one narrow road up the hill. Thinking of the vast quantities of Bass and Alsopp which were fermenting, he wrote 'how we should have enjoyed the beer but... what a relief it would have been for the overworked transport if it had been left behind and biscuit or atta sent".

Gwaler continues to list his problems. The magazine at Darjeeling was small and damp and 'tents come up and not half dozen places in all the country where three belltents could have been pitched together'. Therefore the tents which had arrived at Pankhabari were to be used for storage down there. What in, or how the men slept in the hills he does not say, perhaps he was able to commission the Lepchas to build their quick little shacks.

One can be sure that all these preparations were watched most closely by the Sikkimese who were, however, kept in ignorance of Gwaler's tactics, although opposite the Sikkim stockade, the British were able to work in the jungle, hidden behind a spur. They were by the Rangit river, at the foot of what was to be the Singla tea garden. It was here that Captain Impey was constructing a floating bridge. Made of cane, this was to be assembled on the night of the attack. Gwaler's object was to gain respect and surprise and to force the enemy on to the defensive. He had made it clear right from the start that he would not employ the normal tactics of direct confrontation but would use small parties who could move with ease and approach from behind. In fact his were the guerrilla tactics of the years to come.

When the bridge was ready the soldiers moved. On Thursday four companies left Senchal at noon carrying three days' provisions and one blanket per man. Gwaler joined them at Darjeeling. They marched down the Gok track to the Tukvar spur which they reached at about 5 o'clock. At 1.30 on Friday morning they moved on to the rendezvous. In spite of losing their way, sliding down a precipice and having to cut their way through the jungle, Gwaler writes that 'all was merriment'.

They went down to the river Rangit to the ideal picnic site. Let us pause here, at the foot of what was soon to be Singla Tea Estate and part of the Tukvar Company. At the point where the Chota or Little Rangit and the Rungpo mountain torrents join the Burra or Great Rangit, the valley floor is wide and flat with the forest-clad hills rising steeply all round. It is as if one was in the bottom of a giant's cupped hands. As the Burra Rangit river rushes on to its rendezvous with the Teesta the valley sides close in again.

Through the sand, sparkling like powdered silver, flow rivers of emerald water, dazzling in the brilliance of the sun. The rivers carrying ice cold waters from the glaciers of the world's greatest mountains - such a valley, a land of superlatives. In the waters swim the mahseer fish, much sought after by fishermen, while on the banks are the sunbleached remains of the forest's gigantic trees which the force of water has ripped from the banks during floods. But now with the blue of the pollution-free sky above, the emerald of the rivers and the silver of the sand these sunbleached trees add another touch of magic. Here my family came for my January birthday picnics, to swim in the pools of a tributary of the Rangit, to play in the sand and to count the pug marks of the leopard.

The day over, one faced the ride home on ponies eager to be away from the forest and safe back in the stables. Through the silence of the evening air could be heard the cough of the hungry leopard and the occasional bark of the deer.

45

This stretch of the country has been well described by Hooker. An interesting excursion is via the cane bridge over the Great Rungit 6,000 feet below the station. An excellent road has been cut by which the whole descent of six miles as the crow flies is easily performed by pony back, the whole distance being 11 miles, the scenery being totally different from that of Senchul or even of the foot of the hills being that of a deep mountain valley. I several times made this trip and on the excursion about to be described I was accompanied by Mr. Barnes. I followed the Great Rungit to the Tista into which it flows; in descending from Darjeeling the road is lined with oak, magnolia and chestnut being the main tree and below 6,000 ft tree ferns were widely distributed and palms, 6,500 feet being the upper limit of the palms in the Sikkim Himalaya. The fourth striking feature is the wild plantain which is replaced by a larger species at lower elevations...

... the heat and hardness of the rocks cause the streams to dry up on the eastern slopes and water is conveyed in conduits made out of bamboo split in half. Oak and chestnut are different here. At about 2,000 feet and ten miles from Darj we arrived at a low flat spur tipping down to the bed of the Rungnit at its junction with the Rungpo. This is close to the boundary of the British lands and there is a guard house. Here we paused while the Lepchas constructed a hut, table and chairs.
The spur rises out of the deep valley surrounded by lofty mountains, it is narrow and covered with red clay which the natives chew for goitre and looks down into a gully through which the Rungnit winds through a dense forest. In the opposite direction the Rungpo comes tearing down from the top of Senchul 7,000 feet above, although its roar is heard and its course is visible throughout its length the stream itself is invisible so deep does it cut its channel. The vegetation is a mass of wood and jungle at this point, it is rather scanty and dry with an abundance of sal (one of the main tree types) the dwarf date palm was also very abundant. The descent to the river was exceedingly steep the banks presenting an impenetrable jungle.

When Gwaler and his men reached the valley it was dark. They had to make their way through the steep forest-clad side of the valley and lost their way. However, when they finally reached their rendezvous, all was set for action. Gwaler continues:
Meanwhile Captain Impey had the raft out of the jungle, a Sabundy Sapper crossed the river with a rope and it was only with Captain Impey himself working above his waist in the current that they were able to secure the raft.

It was not until 7.30 am that two companies had been ferried over, Major Maitland fired his signal guns and Gwaler moved on up the hill to the back of the stockade. 'The enemy fled.'

Once within Sikkim they were to receive assistance from the locals and from Chebu Lama. Gwaler was also encouraged to find that the 'resources of the country are much greater than I had supposed. They have brought in onions and spinach, buckwheat and Indian corn, and eggs, some cattle concealed in the jungle - naturally they cannot understand a force maintaining itself. I annexed a list of prices of camp articles of food.'

Gwaler reckoned that it would take ten days to settle everything. And on 28th February 1861 the Hon. Ashley Eden had the Treaty ready. It was signed 'outside the monastery by the Raja' himself and in the presence of all the force. The Treaty was read out by Colonel Gwaler in English to the European troops, in Hindi by the Munshi of the native troops (including the Sikhs), and in Bhutia to the large crowd of locals and the Raja's party. Since most of those present had never seen European troops before they were duly impressed.

Although it was not to last it was, as Gwaler wrote, important because 'The state of Sikkim affords special facilities for opening up relations with Tibet, Western Asia and Central China.' Four reasons were given:

1. Because there has always existed by one section of the people a very friendly disposition towards the British Government and among the remainder of the ruling portion there exists a respect of a very healthy nature.

2. Because it is the shortest and most direct route to Lhasa from British territory and there is already a road from Darjeeling to the Tibetan frontier practicable for pack animals and a pass, the Chola 14,900 feet high open nearly all the year round and free from snow for six months of the year. By the extension of the railway to the foot of the hills the transport of Indian and Indian goods intended to Tibet as well as the Darjeeling tea trade would be greatly facilitated.

3. Because the treaty of 1861 between the British Government and Sikkim establishes free trade between the subjects of the two governments and permission to survey the country and make or improve roads which Sikkim Government are to keep in order if made.

4. Because of intimate connections between Sikkim and Tibet as follows
    a) head of Sikkim is a Tibetan
    b) the mother of the Raja is Tibetan
    c) many of the officials are Tibetan
    d) the Sikkim Raja receives a salary from Tibet

e) the Sikkim Raja together with many officials spends much time in Tibet at Chumbi on account of the close proximity of the Sikkim frontier about three hours from the Tibetan town of Chumbi.

Gwaler recommended that the British establish an embassy at Chumbi as the first stage of sending an envoy to Lhasa and then to treat with China.

There was the possibility of considerable trade with Tibet - gold, silver, musk, borax, ponies, wool, turquoise, silk which would be exchanged for broadcloths, bleached goods, tobacco and pearls.

By 1861 tea was beginning to flourish in Darjeeling and as well as the market in Britain other markets were always being sought not least of which was the Tibetan one, but this being an unknown quantity still was not one of the items listed by Gwaler.

Mr. Halliday's house (c.1880)

48

8

With Bowler Hat and Umbrella to Bhutan

The peace Gwaler and Eden made with Sikkim coincides with Archibald Campbell's retirement and makes a natural break to the pioneering days in British Sikkim. More and more land was being put under tea and the landscape was changing. Some of the early residents either retired or died. Transport to Darjeeling was improved with the building of a new road but with the increase in the population and the export of tea, this improvement was not a recognisable fact. Darjeeling was on the world map, and was growing in size and population.

On the 25th May 1861 Archibald Campbell became a Surgeon-Major and the following year he retired. He was 56 and worn out with his work. He was to die twelve years later before he reached three score years and ten. When he retired, his eldest daughter was twenty; the son, whom Hooker knew as a baby and who was to follow his example, enter the Service and work at Darjeeling, was 14; the youngest of his six children, Harrietta, was eight.

Campbell's achievements are summed up by his contemporary, Mr. Jackson, in one of his reports to the Calcutta desk wallahs:

Whatever has been done here has been done by Dr. Campbell alone.
He found Darjeeling an inaccessible tract of forest, with a very scanty population, by his exertions an excellent sanitorium has been established for troops and others...

Not only did Campbell greet explorers, scientists and scholars like Hooker and the Hungarian, Csoma de Koros, but he also had the pleasure of welcoming important Calcutta visitors such as the wife of the Governor General, Lady Canning who, as an accomplished artist, had long wished to visit and paint in Darjeeling. The actual visit was a happy holiday and a success, she loved the hills and enjoyed her painting, it was all she had hoped it would be. But tragedy struck on her return to Calcutta, she paused to paint in the plains at the foot of the hills, caught the deadly fever and within five days was dead. The British in India were devastated and her husband, who retired in 1862, died almost immediately.

The departure of Archibald and Emily Campbell, with their children, was only one of the changes to take place in Darjeeling society. A gravestone in the old cemetery tells us that George Aylmer Lloyd, CBE, Lieutenant General in Her Majesty's Army, died on 4th June 1865. 76 years of age he died, according to the average age of the cemetery, a very old man.

A few months after Lloyd, another of Darjeeling's pioneers died; on 9th October, Karl Niebel who, as the inscription on his grave read 'preached the gospel for years to the people of these hills', and was one of the Moravians who had first hoped to establish a mission centre at Tukvar but who had retreated to continue his work in Darjeeling.

One of the earliest, if not the earliest, grave in the old cemetery at Darjeeling belongs to a young girl of four years, and one does sadly conjecture that her journey to the new health resort had not only been an ordeal but had been too late.

Alexander Csoma de Koros was another to die before his time, on 11th April 1842. A Hungarian and a famous philologist, he was taken ill on his way back to Tibet to continue his studies of their language. Thirty-three years old when he died on 2nd November 1881 was William Napier Campbell, Assistant Commissioner, second son of the late Dr. Campbell.

While we dwell a little longer in the cemetery we note that amongst many of the young soldiers to be buried in Darjeeling were the first tea planters, one of the earliest being Louis Mandelli, whose work as an ornithologist is every bit as significant as his pioneering work in tea. According to his inscription he was 'appointed by the Italian Government to report on birds of the Eastern Himalayas' and as one of the early landowners, had possessed Commercial Row, now a shopping centre, but then known as Mandelli Gunge. The stresses of life as a tea planter are suggested as the cause of his death for, following in the custom of the time, he was managing several estates and was also part owner of an estate managed by Mr. Martin. Probably the same Mr. Martin, or a relative who had been at Hope Town in its pioneering days.

Another tea planter buried in the early days was John Henry Warren, a name well known in the history of the tea industry, whose memorial tells us that he was held in high esteem by his brother planters and friends.

Along with the rest of India, Darjeeling had adjusted to the new administration. Following on from the Indian uprising of 1857 which did not reach the Sikkim hills, the East India Company had relinquished its control of India to the British Government. All those who had worked hard to convince the Board of Directors of the East India Company that Darjeeling could be and could grow into a town, must have been satisfied. And those Calcutta bureaucrats who sometimes appeared to put every spanner in the works by not supplying enough money for the project of building the station, must have been relieved that the books were now balancing and Darjeeling was set to make a profit! One such to be vindicated was Archbishop Carew, who had persisted in his wish to send the young nuns to begin the convent school which has grown not only into a flourishing school but today has university status.

British Sikkim was preparing for its 'golden years'. In 1864 St. Paul's School moved from Calcutta to the healthier climate at Darjeeling. A Church of England foundation it is, today, a famous public school taking in pupils from all over Asia, the Middle East as well as India. The Rector's house stands on the site of Hodgson's house.

It was from here that Hooker described the width and depth of the snowy mountains and this was where the pioneer, Brian Hodgson had moved to live in a cool and cheap location to be near his old friend from Nepal days, Dr. Campbell. His was a modest bungalow typical of the time. Bought in 1847 from Sir Herbert Maddock who had built it as a residence for himself, the original bungalow had consisted of dining and sitting rooms to the front and two bedrooms with bathroom behind, with a veranda on the front and sides. Of Hodgson, Fred Pinn writes 'he was the former Resident at the Court of Kathmandu until he was 'sacked and 'retired' to Darjeeling. He is one of the greatest explorers of this part of India having explored the history, ethnography, ethnology, languages, Buddhism, natural history and so on.' He was not only a Darjeeling resident but a very great and hard working man.

One morning the tower of the little St. Andrew's Church was found to have collapsed. It was soon after Bishop Cotton had been forced to admit that the church was in such a bad state of repair it should be rebuilt. Then, in spite of grumbles that the church be closer to Jalapahar where the cantonments and most of the congregation were said to live, it was rebuilt on the old site that Napier, or could it have been Lloyd, had decreed in his plan of the town. As Darjeeling developed, with the Chowrasta, the shopping roads and Government House, the church found itself in the centre of Darjeeling proper, Jalapahar being always a 'suburb'. The old St. Andrew's Church had never been consecrated and now there was no-one suitable to lay the foundation stone of the new one. Building went on apace and it must have been a relief when Bishop Milman made it in time to 'lay' the corner stone.

There is no criticism implied in the Bishop's tardiness in coming to Darjeeling. The diocese was so large it was impossible for him to visit all his churches in two years, let alone one. Darjeeling was then part of the diocese of Calcutta and it was not until 1956 that the new diocese of Barrackpore was formed, of which Darjeeling is a part.

The new church was a simple building with no tower - the danger of earthquakes was the excuse, but actually they had run out of money. Government gave one third of the Rs. 31,949 which it cost to build the nave, with seating for 300 people. The rest of the money came from that most generous person, Public Subscription who also provided the organ and the east window. Two beautiful little windows by the font were given by the children of Darjeeling and an altar of red and white Jaipur marble was the gift of a parishioner. There were later additions such as the north and south transepts and finally a tower with peal of five bells.

Tablets on the wall in memory of former parishioners included one to Major General Lloyd, KGB, while the pulpit and reading desk were 'erected to the memory of the beautiful Lady Canning wife of the first Viceroy of India to commemorate a visit to Darjeeling just before her lamented death'.

This tablet to General Lloyd, the founder of Darjeeling, is his only memorial in town, the Lloyd's Botanical Gardens not being named after him. Whatever his disagreements with the old Board of Directors his drive and enthusiasm did much to make Darjeeling happen. In those early days he worked alongside Grant, another man whose contribution tends to be overlooked. Grant alone, with his letters to Calcutta could not have achieved Darjeeling, it was he and Lloyd together who did that. Lloyd left Darjeeling under a cloud, for he seems to have had a tendency to upset some folk. He left the Army, after the 1857 uprising as a General, and retired to Darjeeling.

After Lloyd had left Darjeeling in 1839, Grant, a Protestant, stayed on as Chairman of the Darjeeling Association and was the grandfather of Father Charles Grant, a Catholic and hailed as the Father of the Nepalese Mission.

As was said in the introduction, this tale of Darjeeling will have a European bias and now is a suitable point to stress again that I am guilty of not saying what was done to develop Darjeeling for the Asians who formed the bulk of the population. The area was certainly developing, there was ground being cleared of forest for their farms, ground which was not available for the big tea estates, or the cinchona from which quinine was made. The town, too was developing to serve their needs. There were many shops that would serve all the community but religious needs had also to be met and as early as 1851, the Government gave the necessary land to the Hindus for them to build their temple. The records state that the cost of this very substantial building was met by one man Ranjit Singh, an army subedar employed in the local police force, and he himself assisted the masons in their work. Only Hindus were admitted and the temple, a typical example of Hindu architecture amongst the Victorian buildings, is one of finest and oldest buildings in Darjeeling.

The end of the Sikkim war resulted in peace on two borders but its third neighbour, the Bhutanese, was causing endless trouble. It may be remembered that Campbell left his wife and first born child to go on a mission to Bhutan some twenty years earlier. The Bhutanese had always made every use of the Sikkim troubles and subsequent battles to harry the British. As their confidence increased they began coming into British territory, plundering, massacreing and even removing some of the people as slaves. The pundits in Calcutta, sitting about as remote as an eagle on Mount Everest, decided that the Hon. Ashley Eden, who with Gwaler had been so successful in Sikkim, should lead a deputation to Bhutan to negotiate a treaty and put an end to these raids.

Campbell, with all his experience of these individualistic hillmen, was no longer in Darjeeling to advise, and however much Eden might have been aspiring to high office, he was acquainted with Darjeeling, had worked with Gwaler as the Political Officer attached to the Sikkim Force and should have had more common sense. He had, so to speak cut his milk teeth in the hills and must have remembered how painful, tedious and idiosyncratic hillmen were. He did not draw on Darjeeling's and Campbell's past experience which must have advised him to question the orders of the desk wallahs. Instead he did exactly as he was told, only to find the cutting of his molars a painful and humiliating experience.

The Bhutanese men are tall and muscular. They wear glamorous knee length chubas, which reach down to just cover the tops of their knee-high boots. They carry their straight daggers stuck into their belts and as they walk the skirts of their chubas swing with vigour. The women, with typical mongolian features, cut their black hair short in a sort of pudding basin cut which is both elegant and practical.

When I first saw the Bhutanese en masse they were participating in an archery competition at Kalimpong (now a sub-district of Darjeeling but in 1863 part of their lands, the part they had pinched from Sikkim in earlier times). The setting for this archery match was a field, larger than a football field which had been levelled out of the side of the hill. The Bhutias strode about this field, chubas swinging, arrogant in manner and from time to time shot an arrow from an immense bow to hit a small target. A great deal of noise and shouting accompanied the flight of the arrow.

These mountain men may come of Tibetan stock and be Buddhists, but they are a separate people. Tall and strong they will do nothing by halves, they were, according to some of the early writers on Darjeeling, prepared to work hard but were also independent, gamblers and heavy drinkers.

Anyone who knew the Bhutanese should have known better than to expect them to compromise or negotiate in the western style and should certainly never have regarded them as an irritating nuisance, a mere fly on the little toe of the British Empire.

Armed with obedience, ambition, good intentions, his attache case, and, dare one speculate, his bowler hat and umbrella, Ashley Eden set out for the remote and forbidden kingdom of Bhutan. Like the Amban of Sikkim, the Bhutanese could not resist the opportunity of having such an important man in their mountain stronghold and imprisoned him! That he was able to escape was, perhaps, not just a question of luck but of courage, and determination even though he did return to Darjeeling in the dark like a whipped puppy, his tail between his legs and his tongue hanging out. In due time Eden not only recovered his composure but was sufficiently well regarded to have the Darjeeling sanitorium, when it was finally built for the ordinary European citizen, named after him and in 1877 was appointed Governor of Bengal.

In 1863 Ashley Eden's visit did nothing if it did not encourage the Bhutanese. They did not waste time resorting to meaningless threats, they acted with a surprise attack on an English garrison who added to the humiliation of Eden by abandoning not only the fort but two mountain guns.

Retribution had to be speedy. These noble mountain warriors, with their bows and arrows and a gun they could not use with effect, were no match for the

British Army any more than Sikkim had been. The British did not have to go beyond the first hillock or two and in no time the Bhutanese were sueing for peace and even prepared to cede all the Duars of Bengal and Assam and to liberate all the British subjects. It is apt here to make the point that Britain was doing no more than secure her borders, was not the aggressor and was not interested in acquiring any more of the Bhutanese land than would bring a lasting peace.

It should also be noted that although Britain controlled Bhutan's foreign policy from this time it was not until 1960 that Bhutan opened her frontier to Europeans, before that time only the occasional doctor was able to have access to the country. When carrying a letter to Jigme Dorje, the Bhutanese Foreign Minister it was to his elegant mansion in Kalimpong that I went. In a room, beautiful in its simplicity and elegance, furnished with rich cushions and decorated small tables I was greeted by the Prime Minister himself in perfect English. My stay was short, my mission merely to hand over a letter concerning water rights and rivers. The rivers, and therefore the main water supply, of the tea estates in the Duars emanates from Bhutan. Control of water to the plains of India was also of vital importance to the fantasy plan of some planters to create a British Sikkim, a kind of Switzerland.

Another result of this 1863 Treaty was that Kalimpong joined Darjeeling as a sub-district under British and Bhutanese rule. No tea estates were permitted in this sub-district, that land which was not forest was Khas Mahal land. The town developed its own most interesting identity unsullied by the dictates of the Calcutta fashionable with their aristocratic aspirations.

Even as late as 1955 a visit to the local cinema in Kalimpong to see a cowboy film was an experience. The cinema was small, badly ventilated and smelly. The audience consisted of a few local hillmen, the rest being the burly Tibetan muleteers or their equally burly cousins the Bhutias. They did not need to understand the language, they just loved the action as their cheers and their boos testified.

9

Of Forests and Travel

By 1870 there was peace on all fronts and the administration could concentrate on the development of the District and tackle, amongst other things, the problem of deforestation. It may have a very modern ring to it but it was in 1864 that the Bengal Government inaugurated forestry conservation. The problem with deforestation in the Himalayas goes back even further, possibly beginning in the eighteenth century in Nepal where the population was expanding and the rulers saw wealth in the revenue from land. On the one hand the farmers were heavily taxed and on the other they paid the army with land. This policy created the expansion of the hillsides for cultivation and also led to a large number of landless peasants - and Campbell, whose career had begun in Nepal knew how to tap into this supply of hungry, jobless and landless peasants to man the tea estates.

The first action on forests was taken during the winter of 1862 when Sir Dietrich Brandis inspected some of the Bengal forests, working with Dr. Anderson, the Superintendent of the Botanical Gardens in Calcutta. Proposals for the conservation of the Bengal Forests were submitted and the Government acted with unusual speed, for in 1864 Dr. Anderson, on top of all his other duties took on the forests. This work was to coincide with the Bhutan War but, in spite of that, the first forest reserves were notified in 1865.

As part of the new policy on forest conservation the custom of jhooming - clearing forest by burning of land was discouraged and everyone began to build terraces, both for the tea and for the ordinary crops; cash crops such as cardamom and oranges were also introduced into the Khas Mahal, the land farmed by the hillmen. According to one calculation each hectare of farmland needs 3.48 hectares of forestland to support the farming families. The tea estates were aware of this problem for they were dependent on wood for fuel, building purposes and tea chests, as well as the requirements of the labour and were the first to care for their forests. As part of his annual report the Manager of the Soom Tea Estate wrote in 1891:

> About 900 seedlings of suitable forest trees such as ootis, pipli, cryptomaria - 2,155 bamboo slips and eight maunds of walnut seed planted on vacant land, there are also a quantity of plants in nurseries.

Customs die hard and the practice of jhooming was deep in the Lepcha's culture. Furthermore the British government may have had control of the forests in 'British Sikkim' but could do nothing to prevent jhooming across the border.

Hooker described this practice in his Journal and revived memories for me. He described the excitement he experienced at the beauty of the forest clad hills aglow at night and likens it to the child's excitement at the old 'family' Guy Fawkes Night, the crackle and snap of the bonfires, the sparks lighting up the sky and then the fireworks. I found myself back at Singla, standing on the veranda from where I would look on a dark night across the valley to Sikkim and the numberless red shimmering spots of the fires. It was as if the giants were massed for a party and what one could see was the sparks from their cigarettes glowing in the dark.

The fires were particularly bad one night, in fact my father was out with the men fighting one in the forest which stretched from Singla bungalow down to the river Rangit. As I stood on the veranda with Eva, my mother, we watched the snakes of fires curling their way through the Sikkim forests and while we waited for Malcolm's return we sang a version of the old nursery rhyme, 'London's Burning'. 'Sikkim's burning, Sikkim's burning, fire fire, fetch the water fetch the water.'

While we waited a messenger came with news that there was a fire in the forest further up the ridge, the forest through which our road to Darjeeling went. The factory, the lines (where the labour force had their homes) and our home were surrounded by fire. There was no means of calling for help, no help to come if we could have called them.

More news came in. They were cutting a fire break just below the factory, it had to be the last chance, sparks were already within spitting distance of the thatch on the roofs of the labourers' homes. That the bungalow had a corrugated iron roof was of little comfort when its wooden walls had been partially eaten by white ants and were as dry as tinder.

There was nothing to do but wait, wait and look across the valley to the other fires snaking their way along the hillside. Wait and sing, was all a mother and her five year old child could do.

The fire break worked, factory, homes and lives were saved and the fire beaters went home to sleep, exhausted. The following morning I rode my pony up the hill. The once green forest was nothing but black dust with just the occasional stump and occasional red spark from a log still smouldering with bright red sparks against the charred black of the charcoaled trees and grey ash. The charred forest grew again but that memory of destruction remains.

Most of the early visitors to Darjeeling in the nineteenth century comment on the forests and the trees. Edward Lear, who visited Darjeeling in 1874 describes the forests as well as the scenery and the travelling. At Darjeeling he walked

> by the beautiful path and great trees overlooking inconceivable
> expanses of woody distance and always looking up to remoter heights...

And again on his return from Darjeeling he talks of

drawing at times in that wonderful jungle forest, now millions of times more beautiful than when I came up... The variety and beauty of the foliage above, below and around this descent-road is wondrous! And if the weather prove fine, I can't help thinking of going up to the screwpines tomorrow, if so be they be screwpines, which I doubt, to draw my last inspiration from the soon-never-to-be-seen any more woods of the eastern Himalayas. The bungalow is a wooden structure overlooking a world of forest, a hill, and plain difficult to describe owing to its astonishing vastness.

On January 30th 1874 he wrote from Pankhabari

Quiet and immensity of the scenery; silence of forest. Lovely creepers and cordage, and jungle; bamboos, many dead; hay coloured. Astonishing variety of colours, mostly deep greens, but mixed with yellow green, yellows, orange red and brown. Bananas by the billion. Hollows and basins, ravines and depths. Reach cart road below and arrive at Siliguri.

It was nearly forty years after Lloyd and Grant had been at Darjeeling that Edward Lear was invited to India as the guest of the then Viceroy, Lord Northbrook, and yet the description of his journey to Darjeeling tells us that nothing much had changed in the journey from Calcutta except, perhaps, the train from Calcutta now reached the steamer crossing of the Ganges and that instead of the palkee one travelled by horse drawn 'gharry' on a slightly better road.

January 10 1874 Having crossed the Ganges, Lear and Giorgio arrived at Karagola and go to the dak bungalow where there was no-one who could speak English. There was, says Lear a 'Most wonderful jam of oxen, carts and grain! off at 1 in the dak garry; flat country; avenue of banyans and neems; trees far and near; wonderfully fine trees. Horrid pony struggle, nearly upset, obliged to get out, and was only able to recommence progress by tumbling in the garry (or gharry) as the brutes began to rush on; very disgusting, but 'fate'. A more odious sort of travelling than this, who knows of? Changed fourth time, and the new horse seems about to be like the last. At 5 we are in the cantonments of Purnea... On reaching the dak bungalow, a rather splendid structure, was disgusted to find that no one understood a syllable of English, so having put all the roba inside, I set off in search of allies, and found three Anglos playing bowls. The first was very chilly and advised having a Government garry. The second, one Mr. John Owens, Postmaster, was a brick of the first quality, and came at once and explained about tomorrow's garry time, etc., and arranged for me to pay 48 RS. to Siliguri, I am to stop as I may please at any of the dak bungalows on the road. So I ordered dinner.

January 15. Still misty; no high mountains visible. At noon walked down to Kurseong village, and made a long and large drawing; no good, for there was no sunlight... The Bhutans, Lepchas, or Nepal folk are very cheery and civil.

January 16. Off walking up a pretty stiff ascent, though along a broad carriage road. At certain bends of this road surprisingly fine bits of wood, and rock-girt ravines covered with immensely tall forest trees; tree-ferns also, fern and creepers. The first tree fern I saw was close to the hotel and it astonished me. Morning gray and misty and rather cold; some flakes of snowfall. About 1.30 I think we must have been near the 15th mile, but all now was impenetrable fog. A line of bazaar shops and then a road, right, leading, we hope, to cantonments. After long upward windings, all at once mist clears and shows hideous masses of ugly barrack houses. Meet artilleryman, who says 'Not at Darjeeling at all, two miles farther, should have kept straight on after bazaars.' Again utter fog prevails, houses like magnified coastguard stations looming out of the clouds at intervals. The hideously ugly and scattery condition of this place seems monstrous, but owing to the thick fog, one can know little about it as yet. Mr. Doyle gives us two rooms in his comparatively comfortable hotel... Cold very oppressive, and old Giorgio knocked up by it. I gave him a glass of quinine and sherry and sate him by the fire. Dinner not very bad, but service vile. Giorgio better. I get him a fire in his room and send him to bed.

By the 1870s, the time of Lear's visit, Darjeeling was quite the established centre, catering for travellers, summer residents escaping the hot weather in the plains and those who lived and worked the year round in the hills. Everything still had to be carried up from the plains but the worst of the supply problems, such as the one which had so dogged Sister Gabriel when she could not even get flour for bread, had been solved. By the time of Lear's visit the new 'Cart Road' from the plains had been built, Lloyd's and Napier's road being used only by those in a hurry or when the new road was blocked by landslides as often happened. By 1865 the jail is recorded as having cells for 11 prisoners and cells for four Europeans! The Darjeeling Club was established in 1868 and according to the Gazetteer it was open to 'all gentlemen'. This club had taken over the Assembly rooms. The entrance fee of Rs. 40 after a member had been duly elected was later raised to Rs. 100. The monthly subscription for Darjeeling residents of Rs. 7 varied according to distance from the town. The first President was one Lord Ulick Browne. There were twelve duly elected members on the management committee and the Honorary Secretary was a Mr. M Power.

The Gym Club was descended from the old amusement club, which in its turn had evolved from the old entertainment committee and was taken over by the municipality in 1879 and appears to have had a theatre attached. During this period there was still only one bank in Darjeeling, Lloyd's Bank listed in the Gazetteer. Although Darjeeling had not suffered from earthquakes at this there were sufficient tremors to be a reminder to those building houses that they needed to be substantially built.

As the two decades - 1860 to 1880 draw to a close, travelling from Calcutta improved with the Northern Bengal State Railway being opened for traffic to Jalpaiguri and then extended on to Siliguri. This made way for the final two railways into the Himalayas to be built, a great improvement to a town which had become established in India.

From the advertising pages of the Gazetteer we can glean something of the standard and way of life open to those that could afford it even in a station as far from Calcutta as Darjeeling was. Remedies were advertised, as to-day, for all kinds of minor illness, from headaches to 'diminishing nervous excitement', 'allaying pain', 'procuring tranquillity and repose,' there was also food for infants 'abounding in flesh-forming and bone-forming substances this food perfectly fulfils its objective' - this was taken from an advertisement for Savory and Moores who also advertised 'the safest mild aperient for delicate constitutions, ladies, children and infants and for regular use in warm climates'.

Cutler and Palmers in Calcutta had an extensive wine list including 'Burgundies, Champagnes, Sauternes, German wines' as well as port and sherries not to mention Wachter's 'Plume' Brand which was extra dry and cost Rs.58 for one dozen. Unfortunately there was only a limited supply of liqueurs but perhaps one could compensate by buying 'Kill the Crow' Bitters - a recommended novelty!

Thacker and Spink and Company, Stationers and Printers could provide everything the Darjeeling lady might require, from visiting cards, crests, monograms, ball programmes to ink stands and pen and pencil holders. As well as such mundane necessities as thermometers, drawing instruments and theodolites, there was mourning stationery and nail scissors, sun dials, pedometers and 'Rollup Dressing Cases' most useful for travelling.

Then if one could not find just what one wished to order in Calcutta there was the Indian Agency, of 10 Hare Street, which said 'No list of articles obtainable is attached, because this Agency is prepared to select and supply any and every description of goods and requirements from either the local or London markets and to attend to any and every description of commission.'

And 'This agency has exceptional facilities for securing, on the most favourable terms, packages and chests of the choicest Indian tea as presents for friends at home.' Home, of course meaning Britain!

Darjeeling's various religions were catered for - mention has already been made of St. Andrew's Anglican Church, the Hindu Temple, and the Buddhist Monastery and the Loreto Convent. The Union Church of 1869, for any section of the Protestant church, was in hands of American Methodists. There was some controversy regarding the Brahmosamaj which was built on land given by the Government in 1878, but because no reference was made to the Municipal Commissioners, Mr. Treutler, a Municipal Commissioner and one of those first mentioned as being resident at Tukvar with the Moravian missionaries, felt it necessary to raise an objection.

To protect the residents, the Northern Bengal Mounted Rifle Corps was raised on 6th August 1873 and was absorbed into the Darjeeling Volunteer Rifle Corps in 1881. Most tea planters were members of this Corps, which held an annual training camp in the plains every cold weather. This was soon to become one of the highlights of the social calendar. My mother, Eva Betten recollects that:

> For Malcolm the annual training camp of the Northern Bengal Mounted Rifles provided a welcome break in the Plains. Only once did I accompany him with Ann and Janet when we were allocated a family tent but for which we had to provide all equipment needed. The threat of war was looming, and it was deemed advisable that the women should be able to handle a rifle. We even had a target competition at the end of the week, when I was awarded a silver cup, much to my surprise - I could hit the target!

> To make the journey Ann was carried on a specially made chair with a canopy to keep out the sun or the rain and a little place to protect her feet, she sat facing the way she was leaving. The baby was in a basket, strongly made, also on a coolie's back. We stopped at a godown or storeroom on the way to feed the children.

As well as training for the men and target practice for the women, the camps were great social occasions, with tennis, polo and other social games being played, bridge, mahjong and dancing occupying the evenings. And the richer families who were able to transport real furniture for their 'tents' lived in considerable style.

As Darjeeling grew in size so the necessity for some kind of fire fighting force became essential and in 1872 two manual fire engines were acquired and two Nepali watchmen employed to be in constant attendance and to live on the premises. The engines themselves were manned by a volunteer force. The fire station also had to double as the central point for telephone service.

Even as the shops became established in Darjeeling many women still preferred to have their clothes specially made and, again as Eva Betten records:

> Most memsahibs would employ a Darzee (tailor) who would probably come for two weeks. Some memsahibs who knew their darzees would lend their own sewing machines, I generally preferred the darzee to use his own rather than to ruin mine! He would make the servants clothes,

repair anything that was needed and make the sahib's working clothes as well. He was a very useful man to know.

There was also the travelling barber, known as the knappit ['nappy']. He travelled round and cut the sahib's hair and anyone else's who wanted his hair cutting. With him he carried a very long hollow bamboo with the necessary water in it, if a shave was required at the office or by the roadside. He was very obliging. Normally, however, one asked the houseboy to call the 'knappit' and he would then come at an appointed time. There was one in every estate area and he would go the rounds.

Sometimes, perhaps during the rains the *knappit* would not be able to reach the sahibs on the more remote gardens and, as was the case, when Malcolm was still an assistant and in charge of Singla, the estate down by the Rangit River and the Sikkim border. It was during the monsoon and his hair was growing longer and longer and no *knappit* came. Finally Eva had to set to, to 'cut' her husband's hair! The exercise was not successful. Malcolm fidgeted about and complained that it was not quite right. In exasperation and after the odd warning Eva put down the scissors and left her husband with one side of his head snipped and the other long and bedraggled. He stayed like that till the manager, taking pity on him, used his horse shears to tidy up Malcolm's head until the *knappit* could come.

F.L.B.

Screw-Pine.

61

10

Sikkim in the Nineteenth Century

Edward Lear recorded in his Journal that 'most of the people to whom Dr. Hooker gave me letters are dead, or gone, or ill, or too far off; so that I can go to none'. One man who did make Lear's acquaintance gave him such entertaining company that he left Darjeeling a happier man than he had come. As he records:

> Wrote all day long, barring during a visit from Mr. Assistant Commissioner Ware Edgar, a singularly nice fellow of rough exterior. 'Come and make my house your home.' No. 'Breakfast tomorrow?' Yes. A queer day of application!

This visit had come almost too late to be of real service to Lear or his visit to Darjeeling must have been more lively, for in spite of feeling under the weather this sociable man kept his breakfast appointment on 24th January 1874. 'Went to Mr. Edgar's where, in spite of being but ill able to hold up, had a pleasant breakfast.' The following day he was off, his paintings and sketches of Darjeeling complete. But in spite of his new acquaintance, his departure was fraught with the normal problems of travel.

> January 25. Everything packed and ready; no coolies come. At 8, policeman, but he only stands and stares; I get frantic. At 9.03 coolies come, no rope. Helplessness of these people! 9.30, packs for three made up but no one to carry the remainder; policeman gone again. Intense disgust. Bell of convent singing. Nothing visible for fog. 10, cloud of coolies rush in; some twenty men. Great row! Change luggage! Off!' By the next day Ware Edgar had joined him and the tone of the artist's Journal changes as he records the obvious enjoyment he had with the Assistant Commissioner of Darjeeling.

> January 26. Set off with Edgar and Giorgio down to Kersing, drawing at times in that wonderful jungle forest, now millions of times more beautiful than when I came up on the 14th by its contrast with the vast plains, then hidden. Edgar and I punned bad puns, told stories, and laughed. It is a long time since I passed so pleasant a day, and since I have been in such spirits. Edgar is a singularly delightful companion. By and by the moon appeared and one firefly.

Sad that Lear was only able to record one firefly, it would have been good to have read his description of a host of the tiny creatures. On a good night they so fill the air round one that it is as if the whole of the milky way has come down to enjoy the party and the dancing.

Edward Lear returned to the plains, and no doubt to more grain-laden bullock carts. *The Friend of India's* pages were concerned with the famine and its associated problems, but found space to discuss the annual ice situation which had so concerned it in 1836. The problem, it appears, was caused by the Tudor Ice Company who was unable to get ice from the South Pole or even to build a railway up to 14,000 feet in the Himalayas to get it. The paper concluded its piece on the ice problem by saying 'It is highly discreditable to the British public in this country that they should allow themselves to remain in a state of helpless dependence on North America for their ice.' (*The Friend of India*, 20th August 1874)

Our work is not concerned with either India's ice or famine problems but from time to time we are reminded that they exist down on the plains; it was Grant who dreamt that British Sikkim would be able to grow the much needed food, but nothing much has changed, for now as Edward prepares to say his final farewells to the Himalayas, John Ware Edgar advises him to go straight to Agra on account of the worsening famine.

On 22nd October 1874 *The Friend of India* found a distraction from both the famine and the ice problem to run a confused report on the political situation in the Himalayan kingdoms.

And of late matters have been particularly misty in Nepal, Sikkim and Bootan. Warlike reports and menaces have for the past twelve months filtered down from those little known highlands, Sikkim being at one time the aggressor, now Nepal, now Bhootan... While the Tibetans lately became aware that the Jelap la was unguarded.

Hitherto this rocky gateway has been little used but it is now daily traversed, the Yakla having been almost abandoned. By the former pass Chumbi, in Tibet, is only two day's journey from Renok, and at the foot of the gorge is the monastery Renchengong where the snow and the cold is intense.

The paper rambles on to state that Nepal has sent an ultimatum to Tibet but that the Commissioner, Ware Edgar, would not or could not confirm this. Then there seem to have been numerous communications from Bhutan concerning that kingdom's appetite for saltpetre. The passage continues:

The same ruler also sent Mr. Edgar an unintelligible account of a conversation he had with the Tibetan officials at Phari; relative to a visit which it was proposed Mr. Edgar should make in the cold weather to Sikkim. The Sikkim Raja informed the Tibetans of his reception at Darjeeling, that he expected a visit from a British officer, and that the Governor of India desired friendly relations with the authorities of Tibet.

The Jungpens, in reply, observed that they had constantly heard from their boyhood upwards of expected visits from British officers and that the reports had invariably turned out to be so much chatter.

They did not credit the statements of the present informant, and declined to stultify themselves by sending information to their Government, since the course of events would certainly falsify all such ideas.

Mr. Edgar admits that the meaning of this is unfathomable. It was, perhaps that the Sikkim Durbar were a little uneasy about the scope of the proposed visit to their territory and that they, not caring to evince their private suspicious pretended that the desired explanation was wanted for the benefit of the Tibetans.

Another significant move on the political chess board may be seen in the intention of the Jungpens to remain for a few months at the monastery of Renchengong, already referred to - an entirely novel course of procedure.

Some understanding of what *The Friend of India* meant is gleaned from Ware Edgar's personal journal. It is with Ware Edgar that we again visit Sikkim and the Raja, (the son who succeeded his father after the Sikkim campaign, it was a condition of the peace that the old Raja stand down in favour of his son). The kidnappings had stopped, but otherwise there had been little to no progress in basic relationships between the British Government officials and the Sikkim government since Gwaler had entered Sikkim to teach the Raja his 'first lesson'.

In order to make contact with the Raja, who, like his father before him, was living comfortably in Tibet, Edgar had to go to the border and hope for a successful rendezvous, even though this required him to remain at the whim of the Raja. Cross the border into Tibet he could not, for the Sikkim officials, with the Tibetans behind them, were adamant that no foreigner could pass the frontier. Furthermore they stressed emphatically that no European had ever been to Tibet.

It was at the Jelep La pass into Tibet that John Ware Edgar hoped to meet the Raja. The pass, clearly seen from Darjeeling, is tucked just below, and to the side of, the massive snow covered Kanchenjunga. It was to this bleak place that Edgar travelled, through Sikkim's stupendous scenery, hoping that journey's end, here on the Tibetan frontier, would bring him to a meeting with the Sikkim Raja. There is a small hamlet at Kapup, about an hour's distance from the pass, with the first half mile easy before the real ascent at some rocky zig-zags to the first ridge. The top of the pass is quite large and level but big bare lofty rocks tower up on either side. From the Jelep La pass one looks across to the mountain Hooker loved, the grand snowy mass of Chumolhari with its sugarloaf top, then down to Tibet's Chumbi valley with its scattered villages, while on the Sikkim side a little lake, and the occasional yak grazing, met the roving eye.

Reading Edgar's description of his travels in Sikkim we find it easier to understand why the Raja had had so little an opinion of the Darjeeling district as to give it to the British. As the Commissioner travelled into Sikkim he found himself moving through fertile farms with well established homesteads, the shacks, so prevalent around Darjeeling were no more. Moreover, the further he went away from the border the more prosperous were the farms. He records in his Journal that he camped one night at a height of 5,654 feet in the clearance of a family of herdsmen consisting of an old woman and her children and grandchildren. The old woman was clearly undisputed mistress of everything, although her sons were by no means young men. It was pleasant to see the ready obedience that everyone paid to her orders. He was told that there were over 300 head of sleek handsome cattle in her herd.

One of the old woman's sons told him that a good beast gives six quarts of milk a day and that he valued such a cow at Rs. 35. He said that they supplied butter and a kind of cream cheese to the Darjeeling market. The herdsmen, as well as all the others Edgar met, paid revenue both to the Raja of Sikkim and to the Tibet Government through the ex-Dewan Namguay (the man most responsible for the capture of the two doctors, Campbell and Hooker). The revenue was paid in kind, in butter and cheese to the value of about Rs. 6 yearly to each Government.

Besides this, they were liable to some other demands both in kind and service but these were occasional and not very heavy, though sometimes they had to sell a cow below the market value to the Jungpun or the Sikkim Raja and they had from time to time to make presents to the Sikkim officials. As his travels progressed, Edgar realised that the herd of this old woman, which had, by his standards, been considerable, was not a particularly large one, it being not uncommon for a family to keep a flock of four or five thousand sheep.

While talking with the villagers he was continually quizzed on the British intentions. The people were sure that Britain must wish to extend her territory as far as the fertile Phari valley and even move into Tibet. Of the farming potential of this region there can be no doubt. JW Grant, and the Surveyor Herbert, had recorded the quality of the herds to be found in Sikkim and now, again we gather from Edgar, that the mountains produce a good breed of sheep, ponies and cattle, all of which are superior to any found in the plains of India. The dreams of feeding the starving Indians were not, on the face of it, pure fantasy.

Transport of goods and animals within Sikkim was bad. The tracks or roads were rough and inadequate and the bridges, if there were any, were worse and wheeled traffic was unknown. Edgar considered that bridging the rivers was a priority if trade was to be encouraged, for the rivers, which were often in spate, were dangerous. He himself had once lost a pony as it crossed the Teesta. And traders who had to wait in the steamy, unhealthy valleys for flood waters to subside not only lost animals but picked up fevers. His ideas on roads and bridges were as basic and practical as could be - build the bridges and leave the roads to care for themselves!

Ware Edgar recorded that on Christmas Day he was at the Teesta and not only was the river flooded, but Tibetan traders with forty ponies, besides sheep and cattle, were waiting to cross. They had already waited one day and would have to pass at least another before they would be able to get across. He also met some Tibetan families on their way to Darjeeling, with coarse blankets which they meant to exchange for tobacco. It had taken them six days to cross the Chumbi valley. Families travelled together, with a round trip lasting months and moving at the pace to suit the slowest.

Edgar records the business aspirations of one trader he spoke with who was returning from Tibet. He came from Sikkim and had been away from home for four months. First he had borrowed Rs. 40 at the Darjeeling Bazaar at a rate of 24% per annum. This money had been invested in broadcloth which he exchanged in Tibet for a pony and 250 sheep. When he returned to Darjeeling he hoped to sell the pony for Rs. 50 and as many of the sheep as survived for Rs 3 each.

As well as to establish what needed to be done to improve trade, Edgar had a political mission too, to make contact with the elusive Sikkim Raja. He records that:

After some conversations on different subjects I told the jungpens that there were several questions I wished to discuss with them but that I must first settle about a meeting with the Sikkim Raja which was the main object of my visit. I repeated to them that I had already said to Changzed and the Dewan and asked them to consult with him and to decide on the best thing to be done.

The Jungpen answered with much circumlocution and many compliments, that he was very sorry but he could not give me the necessary invitation to Chumbi as he had received special instructions from the Ampan to meet me on the frontier, to hear all that I wished to say and to report it to Lhasa and the same time explained to me that there was an agreement between Tibet and China that foreigners should not cross the frontier and that no European had ever been allowed into Tibet. I said that, as regards the invitation, I wished him to settle that matter with the Sikkim people, but, that he was mistaken in saying that no European had visited Tibet.

I then told him about the missions of Bogle and Turner and showed him Turner's sketch of the Tishoollama's tomb which he professed not to recognise. The Ex. Dewan took the book to look at the picture which, however, seemed to convey no idea to his mind but, when, on turning over the leaves, he came accidentally on the picture of the temple called Kugopea he at once exclaimed with evident surprise that he at once recognized it and said that Turner's sketch accurately represents the present appearance of the building. The Jungpen was obliged to allow that this was the case and seemed somewhat disconcerted but after thinking through it for a while he said that though he had never heard of Turner's mission, he supposed he had been in Tibet and that I stated that it was almost 100 years since the date of his visit and...

On my return to camp I received a large present of sheep, blankets, butter, flour, salt etc. from the jungpens to whom I gave in return a small musical box and a pair of binoculars. In the evening, as generally happened, a great number of people from the Phari valley collected about my camp fire and we talked about roads, trade, their crops and flocks and herds and other such matters. They went away earlier than usual but after a little while some of the elders came back and after making sure that none of the Jungpen's people were hanging about asked me when we were going to take possession of the Phari valley. They were worried, they said, because of the oppression of the officials and having seen, when on their way to Darjeeling to trade, the prosperity of the countries which we had taken from Bhutan and Sikkim, they were anxious that we should at once annex their country as they had heard we meant to do eventually.

I told them that we had not the slightest intention of taking their country and that it was in the highest degree improbable that we should be compelled to do so but we were very anxious to do what we would to help them by encouraging trade, making roads and bridges and establishing marts but that more than this we could not do. Then they went away, and my people seemed convinced that these people had made this inquiry of themselves, but there is a general belief that we shall eventually annex these Himalayan valleys, and, that their inhabitants greatly desired that we should do so, but I am strongly inclined to suspect that the men were instigated by the Jungpens with a view to sounding me and finding out if there were ulterior motives to my visit.

And in a subsequent conversation I took an opportunity of telling the Jungpens of our great unwillingness to extend our frontiers in any direction and in explaining some of the chief objections to such extensions towards the Himalayas.'

With regard to Tibetan trade and in particular of Tibet's trade with China, Ware Edgar reported that tea was the major import, but it was different from that drunk by the Europeans, in fact Edgar makes the incredible point that China tea was imported into Darjeeling for the consumption of the 'natives' in the district because they could not buy tea to their taste locally. This tea came through Tibet. There was also, it must be noted, a prohibition of the import of Darjeeling tea into Tibet.

Other imports from China into Tibet were silks, porcelain, snuff and articles of luxury. Some of these, particularly the silks, made their way into the bazaar in Kalimpong. It was there in one of the back streets, that I found, in 1955, a small shop full of silk from China. Outside the shop was a dirt track, along which an occasional mangy dog and a few of the mules would stroll. The owner of this shop was proud to display the most sumptuous, and expensive, silk brocades I have ever seen.

I wished for, nay could only afford, a small piece to incorporate into an evening gown, as a memento of my time in Kalimpong, and the expert in this small shop cum stall in the middle of that dirty street, advised me not to buy one of the rich reds which caught my eye, because that is a colour which would not last. The piece that I bought was hand made with a deep blue background, beautiful in its rich intensity, with plenty of gold thread woven in, which adds brightness and depth to the pattern with enough red to create a cheerful contrast. My adviser was, of course right, this material is as beautiful now, as it was over thirty years ago. When I look at it, it is fun to remember and to conjecture. It did not follow the famous silk routes on its journey to Kalimpong but its method of travelling, by mule or, to begin with on men's backs, would have been the same as it had been for centuries. Varieties of brocade are recorded as existing as early as 238 AD. And later when I watched the Buddhist dances in Gangtok, the dancers were wearing old and precious brocade robes. Certainly my silk would have travelled a similar way to the Chinese tea imported into Tibet. It must, however, be noted, that most of the trade from India into Tibet was through Kashmir and Ladakh and not via Sikkim.

Two years after John Ware Edgar's visit to Sikkim the old Raja died and the Deputy Commissioner of Darjeeling proclaimed the Maharaja to be the Raja of Sikkim in spite of intrigue on the part of Tibet. Meanwhile the need for increased trade remained in the melting pot only to be stirred again by Colman Macaulay of the Indian Civil Service in 1882 when he met Tibetan officials at Giatong in north Sikkim. China was involved, there was talk of a mixed scientific and political mission but nothing was to come of it. Lieut. Col. Buchanan wrote of this period:

> This forbearance on the part of the Government of India was, as usual, misinterpreted: the Monks assumed we were afraid of them; a Tibetan army actually invaded Sikkim, built a fort on the top of Mount Lingtu (12,617 feet) and occupied the village of Jewluk on the slope below, a dozen miles and more inside the Sikkim Frontier.

While the desk wallahs in Calcutta were out of touch with the reality of life in the mountains, the lamas in the remote Lhasa strongholds were on their toes against infiltrators to such an extent that those who did cross the border in disguise took not just their lives, but an unpleasant death, in their hands. And any who helped them could also depend on a very unpleasant end. An exceptional band of dedicated explorers, who some might call spies, did, in fact cross the border into Tibet and although it is not the scope nor purpose of this book to follow them, it would be wrong to pass on without a mention of their courage and dedication to duty. Some of them not only began their journeys in Darjeeling but made that town home, one such was Chandra Das, one of the best and most well known. It was the exploits of one of these explorers which inspired Kipling's 'Kim' and his poem 'The Explorer'

Something hidden. Go and find it. Go and look
behind the Ranges
Something lost behind the Ranges. Lost and
waiting for you. Go!

One doubts whether the citybound bureaucrats, sitting behind their large desks in even larger offices knew exactly what they had sanctioned when they reluctantly gave the Surveyor-General permission, and, more to the point, funding, to map the mountains and plateaux of Central Asia. It was all a long way from Darjeeling's pleasant Chowrasta and even further from Calcutta. Captain Montgomerie was working hard and producing results, survey work is mysterious and little understood. Questions were not asked and no-one noticed the comings and goings of the Survey Office's 'holy men'. Trained most carefully by Montgomerie himself, known only by initials, and cunningly disguised, these men, usually, but not always Indians, would attach themselves to traders or other groups of travellers. The flowing robes of the Buddhist monk and the huge sleeves made for an ideal disguise. Rosary, prayer wheel and the pilgrim's staff were their tools. Their professionalism, dedication and accuracy were a credit to Montgomerie's master mind.

They suffered deprivation but no actual loss of life though some of those who assisted them did. The information they gathered was collected, collated and stored. The West learnt that the mysterious Tsangpo river which flows one way in Tibet and another in India was the Brahmaputra. They learnt that more than anything else, including 'chang' (local beer brewed from millet) the Tibetan actually likes and drinks gallons of imported China tea.

One of the explorers was a man known by his initials - as was the custom with 'spies' - as UG, a Tibetan from Sikkim and a teacher of Tibetan in a Darjeeling School. He not only had relations all over the place but carefully fostered them. Cloth, needles, tobacco were carried with him as merchandise as well as medicines and a good supply of money. He left Darjeeling on 9th June

1883. Inquisitive neighbours were informed that he was visiting relations in Sikkim for the Kangsha Festival and he was accompanied out of Darjeeling to Ging monastery by some Bhutia friends. The Ging monastery asked him for the usual present, not just as charity, but to secure success and safety during his wanderings. It is not surprising that he was generous in his gift. From the monastery he descended rapidly to the Rangit river at the bottom of Singla and crossed at the Manjitar bridge. The bridge being closed, UG crossed the river by the ferry raft. He found the heat in the valley excessive but on 12th June he reached Tanggong monastery where his uncle had been the chief lama. He stayed for nine days, joined in the feasting, recruited fresh coolies, laid in a stock of provisions and went on his way.

Having crossed the Rangit they still had to cross the Teesta. It took him and his men two days to make the bridge practicable. He then arrived at a place called Lingmo where he bought a pig, gave half to the coolies and the other half he dried as a present. The feasting this time was in secret, in a cave where his relations from the Chumbi Valley in Tibet visited him, before his real work began, across the border in Tibet. One part of his mission was to make inquiries into the Chinese tea trade to Tibet. From his account we learn that the tea covered great distances from the gardens to Lhasa and there were several stages to the journey which naturally involved many merchants. First the tea was made into bricks which were wrapped in paper before being carried on men's backs to the nearest trade market. Here the paper was removed and the bricks sewn into leather for the yak journey to Lhasa, the next trading post. As has already been said it was a big trade, the Tibetan consumption of tea was phenomenal, every poor man and woman in every destitute homestead had his tea, gallons of it every day. It was a trade the British would have loved to have captured.

Chandra Das, the inspiration for Banerjee in Kipling's 'Kim' was one of the most famous of all the spies. A Bengali, he was a schoolmaster at Darjeeling where he worked with U-Gyen Gya-tso, or UG on Tibetan and Sanskrit literature, some of which he had himself smuggled out of Lhasa.

With U-Gyen Gya-tso's help he secured permission from the Lama of Tashilumpo to visit that monastery where his name was entered as a student and which gave him the opportunity for a series of valuable exploratory journeys which included a long stay in the Holy City. On his return from Lhasa he continued to live in Darjeeling.

RN was instructed to leave Darjeeling and cross the Jelep La pass to the Chumbi Valley. He left on 1st November and accompanied by three trustworthy companions, five permanent Sikkimese servants and five native coolies, crossed the Rangit by ferry. Somehow he survived much travelling and many adventures before he was able to cross back into India and to return to Darjeeling via Gauhati.

PA on the other hand, left Darjeeling on a route which was later to be followed by the early Everest climbers. He went down the ridge which took him past Pashoke and straight to the Teesta after its confluence with the Rangit. He crossed the Teesta on the new iron bridge and climbed up to the Kalimpong bazaar. This route took him to Gnatong from where there are splendid views of the Kanchenjunga range with Kabru and Siniolchum being especially clear and fine. It also enabled him to report on the fact that the Tibetans had built a fort on mount Lingtu (12,617 feet), thereby establishing themselves in Sikkim, and to confirm the other rumours.

In later years, the work of these men who mapped so much of Tibet was found to be remarkably accurate, no mean feat when one considers how they worked. Height was measured by a thermometer placed, quickly, into boiling water, distances were paced and everything had to be recorded in a specially adapted prayer wheel. As well as these men there were European surveyors at work on the Sikkim side. They worked with all the best and most up-to-date equipment in regions where no European had trodden before.

Before the European surveyors could reach Sikkim to do the work they had come to the hills to do they had to pass through Darjeeling. As soon as word got around that the surveyors had arrived in the town they were inundated with requests to survey the new tea gardens, particularly the one at Hope Town. Their real work and interest was further into the mountains and they found Darjeeling something of an irritation.

One of these surveyors was a most dedicated man, Lieut. Harman, who worked up on the remote Donkhya La, the mountain which Hooker describes as being the furthest visible from Darjeeling, and by it is the highest pass into Tibet. This work undoubtedly cost him his life. In those days there was no special survival clothing, nothing specially designed against high altitude, the cold and deprivation. Towards the end of the rains Lieut. Harman left Darjeeling to go north to the snowy ranges and worked as far as the Donkhya pass, 20,260 feet. During this time he was frostbitten and lost four toes. Unable to walk, he had to be carried often by coolies. Sometimes he rode pony back and sometimes he hobbled on crutches. He was in Sikkim for nearly three months and surveyed an area of 1,000 square miles and sketched about 900 square miles of the land at the south east of Everest. The work cost him dear. His health broke down and he retired with his family to Italy but died soon afterwards. At the same time another man, Mr. Robert was also in Sikkim and included the route to the Jelep La pass into Tibet. He covered approximately 900 square miles and was able to report that Hooker's early work had been accurate.

71

11

Agony Point

There was congestion on the road out of Darjeeling, in spite of the improvements made after Colonel Gwaler's Sikkim Campaign of 1860. The increase in traffic was because output on the tea estates had increased from 433,000 lbs in 1866 to 3,928,000 lbs in 1874. The tea, packed in wooden boxes was transported on men's backs, ponies or by the ubiquitous bullock cart along the one road from Darjeeling to Siliguri. The traffic was not one way, the estates imported food and machinery from the plains.

Of one part of this road Edward Lear wrote:

> When I and Georgio were half frozen, we walked some way down the high road towards Siliguri; a novelty to me, nor had I known that there was any road until lately but that we came from by Kalabaree and Punkabaree. But a great deposit of tea boxes, and some two or three hundred ox-carts by the roadside spaces here demonstrate the contrary. The children are very nice, grinning and giggling delightfully, and were they not so dirty, could, being very pretty, be likewise pleasant. Two sets of ladies on oss-back met us, and one Albana in a chair, carried by four men. Dinner quite surprising as to quality; soup, roast goose, fagioli, tongue and brocoli..

As Lear can also testify, the public travelled with all their goods and chattels, it being standard practice in Darjeeling, when renting a house for the season, to bring up everything but the kitchen sink. Says Lear:

> We had to struggle up a long and tough ascent, in the rear of many other oxen-carts. These turn out to be the goods conveyances of a pleasant young fellow named Gompertz going to Darjeeling. I was impressed by the sadness of this young man, as he walked slowly up the steep hill with me; he said, "Happy are you who are going out of this dreadful country in even two years' time!" Little can be said in favour of what I have seen of the landscape in this day's work except as to the woods in the ascent from Kalabaree hither, a bit of Indian scenery atoning for much blank and disappointment. Delicious water here at Punkabaree.

Even as late as 1957, the bullock cart was an integral part of the travel scene in the hills on those roads which were wide enough and not too steep, such as the Sukia Pokri road from Darjeeling to Nepal, or the road from the Teesta to

Gangtok, in Sikkim. These bullock carts always conveyed immeasurable sadness to me, mainly, I suppose, because they were so slow, so plodding and so often along roads drenched in cloud. Never able to hurry, the bullocks walked with heads bowed, eyes sad, the driver sitting huddled in the cold, somehow it had always to be cold, under the hood of the bullock cart. In his hand was a flimsy stick with which to tap the bullocks' flanks as they plodded a few miles a day along the dirt road in a giantscape. These bullocks were Darjeeling's life line. The drivers were earning a living to supplement their smallholdings, or to provide something where otherwise there would have been nothing to eat.

At the beginning of the 1860s, just as tea was taking a real hold in Darjeeling, the industry itself entered a bad patch, suffering from severe growing pains. There had been too many entrepreneurs, too much ignorance and too many dreams of quick easy money.

In the thirty years since CA Bruce was promoted to be Superintendent of the tea forests in Assam and began the first experimental plantations, the world had gone mad, believing that there were fortunes to be made from the tea bush, regardless of how it was planted. Many threw up their jobs as privates or officers in the Army or the Indian Civil Service, postmen to magistrates, all wanted money from tea and all invested their all in Assam. The situation is possibly best summed up in the words of *The Englishman's Overland Mail:*

'The boy fresh from school, who knew naught of agriculture, less, if possible, of horticulture, was pitchforked into a Manager's berth and told to plant tea.'

This madness on the tea estates was exacerbated by those inevitable desk wallahs, this time in London, who were demanding more and more tea.

Demand could only be met at the expense of quality. Today it is only the freshest of the new shoots, the famous two leaves and a bud, which are picked for tea, in those days any leaf, no matter how old would do.

The year 1866 was a disaster in the tea industry, the British public began to demand quality, or perhaps at least something that was drinkable. In 1866 the quality was particularly bad. There was the inevitable crash and subsequent bankruptcies followed by the recognition that first class managers, not just anyone, were required.

Evidence that there was a shortage of suitable managers comes from the experience of Louis Mandelli, the son of an Italian count, who had a part to play in Darjeeling's early tea industry. Fred Pinn has written of Louis:

On the assumption that the "Directories" were checked and compiled before the end of each year, Louis Mandelli could have been at Darjeeling as early as January 1864. He would then have the whole year looking around for 'suitable employment' and at the same time acquiring the basic knowledge of tea culture and the running of a tea garden. There is at any rate, no trace of his having been engaged in any 'gainful' activity in the town. One thing is certain: before the end of 1864 he had landed a contract with the Lebong and Minchu Tea Company as manager of the garden (350 acres) of the same name.

His managerial appointment made him a most eligible bachelor and he got promptly married to Ann Jones at Darjeeling on 21st January 1865 at the R.C. Church. As there is no 'Jones' on the list of Darjeeling residents of any description, it seems most likely that Ann had been brought up from Calcutta for the occasion.

In 1868 (or at the end of 1867) the garden was taken over by the Land Mortgage Bank of India, and a second garden, Mineral Spring (250 acres) was added to Mandelli's responsibility, bringing the total area to 600 acres.

In 1872 another tea garden of 750 acres, the Chongtong Tea Estate, was put under Mandelli's management, bringing the total to 1350 acre. This additional duty must have substantially increased his salary, and he was able - before the end of 1873 - to return his family to Darjeeling, acquiring perhaps at this time the property later called 'Mandelligunge', and to remain on the list of residents until 1878.

Mandelligunge was property in Commercial Row on which such shops as Hall and Anderson, Ltd., Frank Ross and Co, Whiteaway Laidlaw Ltd. were built, and it stretched down to the Post Office Road to include York Villa. It was a substantial property investment and in the very heart of the town.

At first Louis Mandelli prospered and like many others he was speculating. Before the end of 1871 it was recorded that L Mandelli and WR Martin were the owners of Bycemaree, a garden of 70 acres near the plains. This first garden was managed by Mr. Martin, the joint owner. One cannot help but wonder whether he was the son or some relation of the Martin who was at Darjeeling in '48. Whether there is a relationship or not, William Martin made a good job of Bycemaree and the partnership went on to purchase Munja near Pankhabari, but the 160 acres was not considered large enough and this was sold and the larger Kyel Tea Estate of 200 acres bought in 1876.

Mandelli was busy, too busy, his letters to Anderson in Calcutta are a continual tale of woe.

I have three gardens to look to and large ones, and I am in the midst of manufacturing.

I have been away from my place for the last 20 days to another garden under my charge as my Assistant there was doing everything wrong.

This year will be a very busy one for me as the Board at home has decided to alter the articles of the Company into a Tea Company and leave off altogether banking business. To this effect a deputation is coming from home to inspect all the gardens here, Assam and Cachar, value them, report on them etc. etc. You may imagine all the bother I shall have.

Such a year for sickness and bad weather lately experienced, I never saw before... drought at first, incessant rain afterwards and to crown all, cholera amongst coolies, beside the Commission from home to inspect the gardens, all these combined are enough to drive any one mad... Beside I was very nearly losing my wife; she had an attack of cholera, or choleratic diarrhoea, as the Doctor calls it, and you may imagine what an anxious time I had passed: thank God, she is out of danger now and recovering fast.

I have been very unwell and feel I am getting old very fast - This year has been a very bad one indeed for me, both for health and collecting [his birds].

For the past two or three months I have been unwell and troubled with slow fever, cough, deafness etc. etc. In fact I think old age is creeping fast on me: so, you see, I shall have also to take soon a change home.

Whether some of his ill health was caused by the arsenic he used for preserving his birds one cannot tell. Suffice to say he died at the early age of 45 in 1880. His correspondent, a man who had had to take early retirement due to ill health, was Andrew Anderson, Superintendent the Botanical Gardens, Calcutta and the same man who has already been mentioned in connection with the new Forest Commission. Both men were ornithologists and Louis Mandelli was supplying Anderson with specimens of birds.

When the Europeans first came to the Himalayas they were ignorant of their surroundings, everything had to be learnt concerning the flora, fauna and the geomorphology. In this, Louis Mandelli took his part, along with the others who did so much to fill today's text and guidebooks. Mandelli's collection of birds have not only gone to museums at Darjeeling and Calcutta but to the British Museum in London and the Milan Museum in Italy. Some of these Himalayan birds such as the Arboricola Mandelli were named after this Darjeeling tea planter.

As if in recognition of the load he carried, this one manager was to be replaced, after his death, by three men, one for each separate tea estate. It is also interesting to note that on 13th February 1882 he received some monies from Williamson Magor and Company in respect of the Bycemaree and Kyel Tea

Mandelli's rufous-headed tit-babbler (1873) (F. Pinn)

Estates for the season 1881. These monies were most probably in payment for tea leaf which would have been sold as leaf for George Williamson's estate to manufacture. This suggests that Mandelli's gardens were too small to justify building a factory.

Williamson Magor and Company was formed in 1869 as a partnership between James Williamson and Richard Magor, working in Assam, later they were joined by George Williamson. It was a successful partnership which was soon to expand its business to the Darjeeling area. This partnership was now that of Agents of Tea Estates and specific provision was made in the Deed to make advances for carrying on the cultivation and production of tea.

An article in *The Business World* published in April 1989 tells us that the 32 year old Philip Magor is, today, Managing Director of the world's premiere private tea plantation company, George Williamson & Co Ltd.

> With succeeding generations being personally involved in the tea business, it is hardly surprising that the Magors have ended up consolidating their early lead. To day, the family's controlling stakes in a clutch of public companies makes the Magors the largest private tea producing zamindars in the world.

The Williamsons have not survived. The last member of the family, Pat Williamson, remained a bachelor and died an untimely death in 1965. I visited him briefly in his office when in Calcutta with my parents, but was not lucky enough to catch a glimpse of his mongoose which, during office hours, lived in one of the drawers in his desk and would upset unsuspecting visitors by popping his head up to scrutinise them and, no doubt, relieve his boredom.

One of the first Darjeeling estates under the management of George Williamson was Soom, the other was Tukvar where the Moravians had settled. Of Tukvar, Richard Magor, Philip's father and now in semi-retirement writes:

> The story I like about Tukvar is of the assistant who did not like the Burra Sahib of 4 Mangoe Lane (the head office) and prior to his inspection selected an extremely bobbery horse which he stuffed with oats and had someone polishing its saddle to a mirror-like finish. The great man was quickly decanted into the tea and the assistant had to find employment elsewhere but he felt he had won!

Tukvar is no longer one of the Agency's gardens but Soom, next door is. Soom was just a good walk away from Tukvar and when I visited there as a child I found the bungalow somewhat old, gloomy and frightening. Smyth Osbourne the Manager was a good shikar, and had lined the dark corridors with the heads of the animals he had shot. I found it no fun to sip soup under the beady eye of some stuffed animal's head!

Smyth Osbourne also had a collection of shikar photographs which he produced to amuse me after lunch while we sat in the garden, gay with English flowers. One series, in particular, was pointed out to me. It was of a python that he had shot. The first photo showed the dead python with a huge 'pregnant' bulge. Subsequent photos showed it being cut open to display its lunch, a whole deer. It was one of the small Barking Deer that one often heard in the forests and similar to the one we had found as an orphan and kept for a while as a pet. The python had obviously been shot just after he had finished his meal for the deer looked unmarked, not even squashed.

Richard Magor, grandson of the first Magor, records that it was:

> Smyth Osbourne when gharoed by strikers and besieged in the Soom bungalow who rang up Mangoe Lane to say he was just off to lunch at Government House as the strikers gave him permission to attend this important social occasion.

Some years after Lear's visit, in 1881, transport to Darjeeling was transformed with the opening of the Darjeeling Himalayan Railway, called by the Loreto nuns 'the toy train'. According to *The Friend of India* 'The success of the Darjeeling tramway ought to pave the way for similar lines elsewhere.'

The hero of this tramway is Franklin Prestage. It was Sir Ashley Eden, the then Governor of Bengal who sanctioned the scheme in 1878. No doubt as he put his seal on the railway, Eden remembered his days as a Political Officer in the

Sikkim campaign and the frequent, sometimes frantic letters he had received from Colonel Gwaler as he struggled with the problems of transporting provisions into the hills, with the single, steep and narrow road.

Prestage was sure that a line, however expensive to build, would pay its way by cutting the costs of bullock cart transport between the plains and Darjeeling. Rice, for example was Rs. 98 a ton at Siliguri and Rs. 238 at Darjeeling and even more by the time it reached the tea gardens. He was proved right, for within six years the small railway was halving the cartage rates, taking four-fifths less journey time and also, important for the shareholders, paying 8% dividends. And, according to my understanding, it was a woman, Prestage's wife, who enabled him to solve the tricky problem of gradient by corkscrewing up the mountainside! Many thought the plan crazy, but once completed, the little railway was hailed as an engineering miracle.

One of those to go on the payroll of this railway was Louis Mandelli's eldest son, also a Louis. He was in the audit and traffic branch; as a travelling inspector for accounts and, no doubt because the railway had no house for him, he is recorded as staying with his father's partner W Martin, on the Kyel Tea Estate in 1890. Later he was the stationmaster at Darjeeling, retiring in the 1920s, probably just before my father first went out! A grandson who used to visit him regularly wrote to me saying:

> Yes I loved Darjeeling and always looked forward to the little train journey and its final effort to make the 'loop' before dropping down to Darjeeling. We played the local boys' game of jumping from the train as it climbed the up curve of the famous 'loop' and running to catch the train before it gathered speed on the down curve. My mother used to have forty-fits in case we were left behind!

For travel on this line one was advised to get to the Darjeeling train early on arrival at Siliguri in order to reserve a seat, while fellow passengers on the overnight express from Calcutta rushed to get to their breakfasts first. Better to have a cold breakfast, for a seat with its back to the engine ensured that one had no blown smuts filling the eyes on the seven hour journey to come. It was also advisable to take a coat, however hot it felt in the plains, it was always cooler up in the mountains.

Describing it as one of the engineering miracles of the 19th century, Arthur Dash says:

> The only railways in the District are those of the Darjeeling Himalayan Railway, a two feet gauge steam tramway system, consisting of the main line from Siliguri to Darjeeling, and one branch line along the Tista ...

> The main line starts from Siliguri, 398 feet above sea-level, and runs along the Hill Cart Road for about 7 1/4 miles on the level to Sukna.

After this station the railway begins to climb the Himalayan foothills at an average gradient of 1 in 20 reaching its highest point, 7,407 feet above sea-level, at Ghum station, 47 miles from Siliguri. It then descends for about four miles to the terminus at Darjeeling Station, 51 miles from Siliguri and 6,812 feet above sea-level.

For most of its length the railway runs along the Hill Cart Road (the 1861 road), though diversions of the rail line from the road, in search of easier alignments, are frequent enough. At places on either side of Ghum, the road negotiates gradients much steeper than the average, and those difficulties of ascent are overcome by ingenious devices. One is the loop where the line passes through a tunnel, runs in a complete circle and over the roof of the tunnel again, so that the alignment follows a large spiral. Another is the reversing station where the train is shunted backwards on an ascending gradient for some distance, so that the alignment climbs the hillside in a zig-zag like a hill footpath. The contour of the hill-sides provides many special problems in alignment for a railway which, at many places, has to negotiate curves as sharp as 60 feet in radius.

The 'toy train' on the loop (c.1910) (Johnston & Hoffman)

79

...The rolling stock is necessarily small. In the early days of the railway, passengers were carried in open trollies, fitted with hoods and curtains for protection against bad weather, but now they are carried in bogie rolling stock measuring 24 by 6 feet. The new first class carriages are fitted with large plate glass observation windows, enabling passengers to obtain an uninterrupted view of the scenery.

As the train twists its way up the hill, the passenger is treated to breathtaking views. Spice is added to the drama of the scenery by the swaying of the carriages. For safety reasons the track had been cambered to face inwards to the hillside, but the motion of swinging as the train rounded each bend only intensified the apprehension of the nervous passengers. The width of the carriages is over three times that of the rail gauge giving, from time to time, the sensation of travelling over the edge of a precipice.

The most dramatic spots were given names, which were painted on boards and displayed, such as 'Sensation Corner' 'Agony Point' and 'Mad Torrent' also known as Paglijhora. But a Governor Inspector, with more sense of duty than humour (not Mandelli), doubted the wisdom of calling the timid passengers' attention to their apparent, rather than real, danger, and the boards were removed.

The best route for the train was obviously the same as that chosen for the final road in 1861. With the improvements to both road and rail in modern times there are now a total of 132 level crossings between Siliguri and Darjeeling, as tarmac and iron haggle for the best position on the cliff side!

This little 'toy train' played an important part in the economy of the district at all times but during the Second World War there was an increase in both passenger traffic, troops going on leave or convalescence, goods traffic and the necessary provisions for the town. The line coped.

I once boarded this train for the short trip from Ghoom to Darjeeling. I am glad it was no longer. It was the end of a journey best forgotten. Our old and tired car had been pushed into Ghoom. My father stayed with the car and the rest of the family had then to make the best way they could into Darjeeling. It was a dark, cold night, the road back down to the bungalow was through the forest where both leopards and bears dwelt. We could only go on! There was one taxi, it already held some passengers but was prepared to take my two elder sisters. It would have taken us too, for the money, if we could have squeezed ourselves in. So it was that my mother and I waited the arrival of the last train of the day. When the train chugged its way into the station only a few passengers alighted and the train, with its miniature carriages was full. We found a cranny. The carriages, of course, are small, it is only a 'toy train'. Our carriage was full, people, belongings, babies and chickens filled every available space. We were glad the journey to Darjeeling was short and that we were on our way.

12

Towards Tibet

After twenty years of peace in Darjeeling, trouble broke out on the Tibetan border towards the end of the 1880s. Tibet, backed by China, hoped to restablish its hold over Sikkim. The leading lama class in Tibet and the great traders, who had the monopoly of trade in China tea, viewed the road to the Jelep La, which Ware Edgar had built, with apprehension. Their concern was aggravated by an over enthusiastic member of the Indian Civil Service, one Colman Macauley, who allowed himself to be impressed by a minor Tibetan official who told him that the Tibetans would welcome trade with Britain. To make matters worse Macauley, with Chandra Das as his interpreter proposed to go to Tibet. The man the Tibetans hated above all other men was Chandra Das who had infiltrated across their border and worked as a 'spy' in Tibet. This business of Macauley's lit one of those sad sparks whose subsequent explosions changed the course of history. In 1886 Macauley's 'friendly' mission, which, incidentally, included 300 troops was called off but it was too late, the Tibetans had taken fright.

Meanwhile the Sikkim Raja, under the influence of his new Tibetan wife, had taken up residence in the Chumbi valley, in complete violation of the 1861 treaty which required him to reside in Sikkim for nine months of the year. And, while the tensions grew, so did Tibetan influence in Sikkim.

Tibet made the first hostile move by sending a large troop of men across the border to occupy Lingtu Mount, on the Sikkim side of the border from the Jelep La. The explorer KG confirmed that the Tibetans were there when he slipped quietly over the Jelep La to do his secret work.

The 2nd Regiment of the Derbyshires was the regiment despatched to deal with the infiltrators. Compared to Gwaler's Sikkim campaign their journey into the hills was easy. We are told, casually, as if travel from Calcutta had never been a problem, that the soldiers had taken the train from Calcutta to Siliguri with slight delay at the Ganges due to having to unload their baggage onto the steamer, there being no bridge then across the river. They arrived at Siliguri on the afternoon of 7th of March 1888. Here they had to sleep 'in huts of bamboos because their tents had gone on to Pedong - four marches on.'

They spent a day in Siliguri playing with their baggage and the mules because 'all old campaigners know the advantage of loading and unloading baggage and so preventing frequent halts to load and re-load beasts, besides preventing sores to mules and endless trouble!' The extra day at Siliguri also enabled the Viceroy of India, Lord Dufferin, to inspect the troops as he passed through on his way from Darjeeling to Calcutta.

This more direct route into Sikkim along the Teesta Valley had not been available to Gwaler since the Kalimpong subdivision was not acquired until 1864.

The soldiers who chose not to take the train from Siliguri to Darjeeling, preferring to march the Teesta valley route to Kalimpong were not beset with the communication problems that had so worried Gwaler. It was as well that the first stage of their journey was easy for once in the mountains it was a hard march to the Jelep La.

The Derbyshires left Siliguri at 5 am to march along a level road used by the tea planters. After seven miles they entered the Terai, the belt of forest which extends for hundreds of miles along the base of the Himalayas. The grass on either side of the road had been burnt and as they marched, the regiment were covered in black ash. Then the scenery changed and they found that the jungle through which the road had been cut was dense, there were tall leaves and the immense trees were covered with orchids. Elephants, tigers, bison and all sorts lived in the tall, concealing grass.

Their first camp had been prepared for them by the PWD who had built dry weather shelters out of bamboo to enable the tents to be sent on ahead to Pedong. Not expecting any rain at that time of the year, these huts had only been roofed with bamboo, which failed to keep out the rain which fell during the night. They were all soaked.

Camp Sivok, situated at the debouchure of the river Tista and surrounded by the densest forest being about as jungli a place as one could wish for. The river Tista is here a deep rapid stream about 150 yards wide, the waters are greenish and very cold. Every man had a cold wash, swimming was forbidden as being too dangerous but also the water was too cold.

They had a good, 12 mile march the following day to Rongli where more dry weather huts were awaiting them.

The march along the Teesta valley was described as very beautiful with 'Jungle Cock screaming defiance to his enemy across the valley.' A 'sylvan scene to rouse a naturalist or an artist's fancies.' The narrow, gorgelike valley was steamy by midday. The hills rose precipitously on both sides. But the men were in fine fettle when they reached Rongli and the officers were most hospitably entertained by a tea planting gentleman. There was more rain, but this time they were prepared and they kept fires alight to keep off malaria as it was considered to be a most feverish looking place.

Years later I described the same route as seen from a car window at about the same time of year as the Derbyshires were passing through:

We had the most wonderful run down going along the bank of the Tista for an hour. This in a tremendously deep gorge with the forested cliffs rising for three thousand feet on either side. The river, which, even at this time of the year, when it is low, flows at a terrific speed, was a lovely deep clear jade, and in spots it appeared not to be moving at all. At one place we saw a tributary coming down in a shady valley and it was a real deep prussian blue, almost black. The truth is that living in the wonderfully magnificent scenery that I am doing at the moment it is so easy to fail to appreciate the real value of each successive magnificent view, but the road by the Teesta to the Coronation Bridge (Camp Sivok) is incredible. I had always considered the Anderson Bridge at Pashoke beautiful but compared to the Coronation Bridge it is paltry. Here the gorge is really stupendous and the white bridge, in a lovely sweeping design must be nearly 100 feet above the river with the elegant, stilt like legs going down. Soon after crossing the bridge the road comes out into the plains.

While wandering along the banks of the Tista it was mostly very rocky, except in places where it was sandy and here we would see the pug marks of several animals, those of the deer keeping close into the rocks while those of the leopards and tigers going boldly out, there were an incredible number.

The next day the Derbyshires left the Teesta valley for their first day of hill climbing, six miles along the Teesta was fairly level, then the suspension bridge and the cart road ceased. This was 710 feet above sea and they now had to climb to Kalimpong, 3,200 feet 'which did us a lot of good in getting some of the yellow fat off. Last part of the road was bad and the sun was hot, we were in camp by noon.'

Captain Wyley continues:
Kalimpong is a place of some importance in British Sikkim, there is a large weekly market there on Sundays and also a missionary establishment, we found the bazar in full swing on our arrival and tommy was able to provide himself with fresh eggs, milk and butter galore.

Again in my description of the place I wrote:
Kalimpong is a trade centre and the place was full of wild and woolly Tibetans who had come in with the mule trains. We saw a piece of ground about the size of two football pitches packed with mules and Tibetans. There also was the largest straw stack I have ever seen. It was easily 20 feet high and they were still building it, two more cart loads

The Teesta valley (1940)

of rice straw were arriving on site. We passed several godowns
(storehouses) oozing with wool. There were also several carts pulled
up at the side of the road laden with raw wool. As we went on we came
to another open space where there was an archery contest on foot. The
target was a good 200 yards from the contestants and when the arrow
landed on the target they yelled. I should think there was every type of
person there, Nepalese, Lepchas, Sikkimese, Bhutias, Tibetans, Chinese, Bengalis, Punjabis and Europeans.

The troops made an early start for Pedong, but their luck was out for they
make no mention of the view of the mountains from Kalimpong, which must have
been, as they often were, hidden behind the clouds. Of the Kanchenjunga range
I was to write:

> This morning I saw the most wonderful sunrise on the snows. Though
> I have been at Kalimpong a week it is the first time that I have seen
> them, and because one is seeing them from a different angle and
> elevation they don't look like the same mountains that we see from
> Darjeeling except that they are as beautiful. The snows themselves
> actually face to the north so that the sun is reflected on them. This
> morning all the intervening mountains were covered with mist, a very
> beautiful soft white friendly mist and poking up above these, as if
> floating on the mist were the mountains.

The Derbyshires would have had an enjoyable 20 mile walk along a
pleasant wooded, rather than dense forest track, to Pedong. It was here some
Catholic fathers had set up a remote mission. It was here they met up with the
advance party and their tents. Next day they dropped into the valley of the Rishi
and having crossed the river they faced a 10,000 feet climb up to meet their foe.
A few years later this route was described as being 'not so much a road but a
steeply inclined causeway of big flat stones.' This was surely the land of the
giants for a soldier who toiled up the mountainside likened it to the leg of the table,
since Tibet had been described as being a tableland. Before they reached the top
they came to a small village where there is a big black rock on which someone
carved the letters 'C.I.N.R.A. 21.3.88'.

The army built a camp in a hollow from which they had a splendid view
on three sides - right in front was a path going up to the top of Mount Lingtu
(12,617 feet) where the Tibetans had built their fort. To the north lay the massive
Kanchenjunga group and to the east and south the hill Gipmochi (14,532 feet),
the trijunction point of Tibet, Bhutan and Sikkim; on the other side was the Mo
Chu valley running through Bhutan to the plains below and the obvious route for
the railway which was never to be built. As early as 1881 the Calcutta Press had
reported that the Russians had completed their railway as far as Kigil Arrat in
Turkistan.

So much effort and loss of life for so little. The 'fight' with the Tibetans was hardly a skirmish, so much for the rumours! A nation which fights with swords and bows and arrows against artillery can have no resistance and it was over almost before it had begun. Then the Amban said he wanted peace but all was delay and the British did penance as they waited a long, cold wait up by the Jelep La. Finally the treaty was signed and the British army moved out leaving a scattering of isolated cemeteries as they went. In the highest one is the tombstone to the soldier who got lost on the pass and was frozen to a lonely death. A trade mission was established in Tibet, links with Tibet, Kalimpong and Darjeeling were forged. But nothing of substance was achieved. The suspicions of the Tibetans, the British fear of the Russians and the success of the Chinese diplomacy remained the real and unresolved issues.

The next Viceroy of India was Lord Curzon. Both he and the British Government in London suffered from Russiaphobia and were convinced that the Russians had eyes on Tibet. Sitting in their urban offices and distanced from the reality of the mountains they could look at a map, wish for Tibet and be convinced that the Russians were all set for a conquest. The inhospitable vastness of that high mountain kingdom was its defence. The goal to reach Lhasa remained to tantalise all, a challenge every bit as exciting as being the first to reach the South Pole or to climb Everest. Chandra Das and the other Indian explorers were not the only ones to slip, disguised, across the border.

The Rongpo bridge into Sikkim (1955)

13

The Victorians

The narrow gauge railway from Siliguri to Darjeeling put the district on the map and enabled it to be included in Thomas Cook's annual World Tour.

The town had just about everything that the Victorians could wish for - a race course, polo ground, billiard rooms, small theatre, assembly rooms, ballroom, clubs and a roller skating rink with tennis courts. There were schools too, to suit most tastes, colours and religions, especially the various Christian fads and fancies. The Anglicans, at St. Paul's, were up at Jalapahar. St. Joseph's, down at North Point, was run by Canadian Jesuit fathers who had taken over the boys' school, which the Loreto nuns had set up, but the nuns retained the very young boys.

Sister Gabriel, one of the first of the pioneering nuns of 1848, the trojan who had kept them all cheerful through those difficult early days, was still going strong and looking forward to greeting the 20th century. Life at the Convent was very different now, water no longer had to be collected from the stream at the bottom of the garden and flour for bread could be bought, to mention just a few of the improvements.

Above the Convent, the hill leading up towards the Shrubberies, now Government House, and the Chowrasta where the band played, was sparse woodland. This is Birch Hill and in among the trees dwellings and gardens lay, as now, partially hidden. The Convent itself lies facing the view of the snows just below the cart road which leads from the station and the main bazaar to the Lebong Cantonments, and the Darjeeling Race Course, where the little Tibetan ponies are regularly raced. This road follows the contour line along from the bazaar. Further along this main road from the Convent one comes to St. Joseph's College at North Point. It is here that the house Singamari, destroyed in the 1897 earthquake, and rebuilt, was turned into a school with Miss Webb, a member of a well known Darjeeling family as Head Mistress, during the Second World War.

At North Point a rough track drops abruptly away through some thin forest towards the American Methodist school, Mount Hermon, earlier known as Queen's Hill School for Girls before it became fully co-educational. Going on past Mount Hermon, through Patia Bustee and more forest, the road drops almost sheer down to the turning to Soom tea garden before passing the two Tukvars and Barnsbeg. After some forest, it branches again, with one track heading for the Burra or Great Rangit and Singla Bazaar, and the other to the bridge across the

Darjeeling Bazaar (c.1910) (Johnston & Hoffman)

Rangit into Sikkim at Manjitar. This road was classified as a fairweather road only!

Returning back towards Darjeeling, there were other schools too; there was the Maharanee School, Oak Lodge, a free day school for Bengali children; and the Bhutia school, later combined with the Zillah school, also took some boarders. The Diocesan Girls' High School was built in a pretty wooded site on Birch Hill and was under the Sisters of the Community of St. John the Baptist of Clewer - all trained teachers.

By the end of the 19th century there were numerous boarding houses as well as hotels, such as the Woodlands Hotel, whose guests included such grand people as Earls and Countesses, Princes and Lords as well as various other members of the nobility. The Rockville Grand Hotel was under the same management as the Woodlands, with similar rates and but half a mile from the station, with two good routes, the shortest one being too steep for rickshaws. And, of course, of its views.

The Central Hotel, by the Post Office was three fifths of a mile from the station and was four storeys high on Mount Pleasant Road side, and just one storey high on the Post Office side. The Dramdruid Hotel was a similar distance from the Railway Station and boasted a large drawing room. Sunnybank, on the other hand was a boarding establishment for ladies, lady boarders and children only, while Jones Hotel boasted that it kept the best stables. French, German, Italian, Dutch, Spanish and English were all spoken at Alice Villas by the manageress.

Visitors were not advised to visit the Post and Telegraph Office which was a two storey building set in a hole in the steep hillside, to enter one first crossed a wooden bridge to the veranda of the upper storey where there were primitive letter boxes. To enter the main office one had to go through a trap door in the veranda and descend a ladder to the telegraph office window where, 'you have difficulty in finding sufficient room to write out your telegram'. By mid-day the upper veranda was crowded with chaprassis and dakwallahs waiting for the mail, and it was not often possible to gain access to the trap door.

There was a very European shopping centre in Commercial and Mckenzie Roads and along one side of the Chowrasta. ...Whiteaway Laidlaw & Co. Drapers; then Commercial Lane branches off with Mrs. Jones, Confectionery at the top, Mrs. Ottewill, Milliner; Partridge, Chemists; Hall and Anderson, Drapers; Mitchell and Company, Tailors; Broom, Sporting Goods; Newman and Co. Booksellers and Stationers; Rollington Smith, Photographers. The only building on the left was Ottewill's Music Shop, where the road sloped down steeply to pass Bayer's Confectionery shop, a few further paces to the cross roads, a sharp turn round to the right, a few more paces, then sharp round to the left, and down Lloyd's Road, where the bank of that name was. This road zig-zagged down to the Cart Road and northwards into the Market Place to the Hindu Temple....

The various guide books made frequent reference to the 'Children's Pleasance', a children's play area which was enjoyed by children of all races and creeds. Those visitors with social aspiration found that Government House was only three fifths of a mile from the Chowrasta and just off the West Mall.

Passing through these gates you find a small building on the left in which the Visitor's book is kept. In this you enter your name, address in Darjeeling, occupation and date of departure if you wish to pay your respects to his Excellency the Governor. Strangers should not go beyond this point without an invitation.

The building was described as being 50 yards north of the gate. It is a picturesque two storey house built in rustic style in 1879. This site was originally granted to a Mr. Edward Hepper in 1840 who transferred it to Thomas E Turton in September of the same year. The latter gentleman appears to have built a house called Solitaire which was removed in 1878 to make way for 'The Shrubbery' or Government House as it is now called.

For those Europeans requiring medical attention there was the Eden Sanatorium. Half a mile from the station, it was built on a knoll jutting out from the west side of the main ridge, and overlooking the town and the whole side of the western valley with fine views of the snows. It was a large, Victorian building, opened in 1883 and named after Sir Ashley Eden, whom we met as a young man in Sikkim and then Bhutan and who was one of the Lieutenant Governors of Bengal. It was his drive which had done much to make the sanitorium exist. The building was equipped for the normal amusements of the convalescents, with a billiard room and tennis court. It is also to be noted that there were a number of free beds maintained by subscription. Also to be noted is the fact that 'the kitchens and pantries are tiled and English cooking ranges are a feature of the institution. Catering is excellent and the grounds are spacious and well laid out. It is open from March 10 to November 15.' There was an up-to-date hospital near by.

For the Asians requiring medical facilities there was the Lowis Jubilee Sanatorium just one fifth of a mile from the station. 'The first building on the right is a recreation hall which contains a good library.' The cost for staying there was Rs. 4 for Orthodox Hindus and Rs. 5 for general patients. The sanatorium, having been built for 'natives of India', was opened in 1888. Funds for the building were placed at the disposal of Mr. Lowis by the late Maharaja Gobind Lal Rangpur and the land on which it stands was given by his Highness the late Maharaja of Cooch Behar.

The season in Darjeeling began at Easter when the Calcutta folk and the Bengal Government arrived and closed during September, though many left when the worst of Calcutta's heat was over and before the monsoons. The schools had a nine month term with three months' Christmas holiday. And during

October and November the private and commercial residents, the tea planters, the administrators and many others who spent the winter in Darjeeling were able to enjoy the perfect views, blue skies and sunshine without the inconvenience of the Calcutta folk!

Regular visitors to Darjeeling were the Hindu family of Bonnerjee whose ancestral home had been in Kidderpore, a suburb in Calcutta on the river Hughli. A visit to the hills is recorded; 'During the Easter holidays of 1894, the Bonnerjees went to Darjeeling for a short visit, and Milly and the other young people were greatly thrilled with the views of Kanchenjunga and the Himalayas. They stayed in an annexe of Woodland's Hotel. They had been to Darjeeling before in 1886 but remembered nothing of the visit, so this was really their first sight of the Snows, which were to become so familiar in later life.'

A few years after Milly's marriage with Amiya Nath Chaudhuri (or Omi) they decided in 1919 that:

> Instead of renting a house in Darjeeling every year for their annual holiday, such houses not being always easy to come by and by no means always comfortable, it would be a very good thing to buy a house of their own. Since 1917, they had taken the same house every year, 'Edelweiss' a large and convenient one some way below the Chowrasta or Mall, the centre of Darjeeling. But in 1919 this house was sold. At the same time a very fine property was up for sale. Two houses had been built in modern style by a firm of American dentists, Smith Bros., who had been working for some time both in Calcutta and Darjeeling. One partner was now retiring, and the firm decided to sell his house and also the other one, which they would rent from the purchaser. The partners' house was called 'The Wigwam', just off the Chowrasta. Being built against the cliff side, the front door, entrance lobby and large drawing room were at street level. On the next floor below were two good sized bedrooms, bathrooms and a separate lavatory with modern sanitation, then almost unique in Darjeeling. On the lowest floor, there were a large dining room and kitchen. The house had central heating, hitherto unknown and undreamed of in Darjeeling, while the drawing room had a beautiful wooden parquet floor. All the rooms had large windows with glorious views of the surrounding hills. Being just off the Chowrasta, the house was quite secluded and not overlooked and yet three minutes from the Chowrasta shops and five minutes from the Gymkhana Club, the great meeting place of all Darjeeling holiday makers, as well as of the Government officials who came up to Darjeeling during the hot weather. Omi and Pramila decided that with the addition of an annexe on the dining room floor level, containing two more bedrooms and a bathroom and lavatory, the house would hold them all. It may be mentioned here that Omi had been eminently successful in his profession and had become one of the

leading barristers at the Calcutta bar, so he was in a position to buy the house and all the family, especially Omi, became very fond of the place and spent every holiday there.'

They never changed the name of the house, 'Wigwam', because it really was a delightful house with a gorgeous view. When father bought the house, it was suggested to him by some busybody that he should change the name. Father produced a dictionary where 'Wigwam' was defined as an 'Indian dwelling' and said that though the Indians living there were a different breed they were Indians all the same! The 'Wigwam' it remained. The adjoining house was called 'Dantkoti' or Tooth House by the original owner. Father didn't change the name of this either but let it to a dentist.

As the 19th century made way for the 20th, the Calcutta newspapers employed a regular Darjeeling correspondent.

Extracts 'from Our Correspondent, Darjeeling', during June 3rd 1897. The weather has held up wonderfully since I last wrote. It has allowed of outdoor amusements including cricket and football. St. Joseph's College met the Darjeeling Cricket Club and beat it by some 50 runs and St. Paul's School beat a strong team of planters by over 100 runs. The Mountain Battery played the Jalapahar Depot at an association game of football and were the victors and no wonder for they are a splendid body of men with all the vigour of health and strength whilst the Depot are invalids seeking renewal of both. There was another game at Lebong last Wednesday between a strong team captained by Mr. Clarke of St. Paul's School and the Manchesters - it was the best contested game this season and was won by the Manchesters.

Among the new arrivals are Mr and Mrs. Claude White from Sikkim and Lieutenant Perreau of the Worcesters from Dum Dum. Mr. White has not been very well and has come in for medical advice. There have been a few changes among the planters Mr. Len Bill has gone from Banockburn to Central Terai, Mr. Pollock of Pandam has resigned and returned home and Mr. Pritchard has left Dhoteria.

The Following were the first ties of the Billiard Handicap.... The fourth tie has yet to be played and Mr. Allen is favourite.

The birthday ball at the Shrubbery (Government House) on the 26th was by far the best and nicest of any this season. Lady MacKenzie, always amiable, surpassed herself in courtesy and attention to her guests and Captain Ross, the A.D.C., himself a dancing man, and a much sought after partner, cheerfully sacrificed his own pleasure to administer to that of others by making people acquainted with each other and seeing that the ladies did not lack for partners. The band was Cotta's from Calcutta and the supper and the wines were of the best. There were eighteen dances and extras and the guests did not disperse till about 3 a.m. And all left with a feeling of regret that a pleasant evening had come to an end.

The want of a band to play out of doors is very much felt just now especially with the glorious summer afternoons we have been having when every inch of room on the seats of the Chawrusta has been filled. There is a pretty bandstand there but there has been no band until last Saturday when by the courtesy of Major Kinghall the band of the Depot, a scratch one, made up of a few invalids from different regiments have played in it as an experiment to ascertain whether our love of music comes as high as our pockets. We had a volunteer cum town band for many years. It was a poor and inexpensive one and after a long struggle for existence it had to be disbanded for want of support from the public. Its chief help came from the Amusement Club and its members and they found that they were maintaining a band for the benefit of the public which gave little or nothing so they withdrew their help and the band ceased to exist. The club now imports a string band for its own use every season.

The Dorje band is to play out for a few more Saturdays and it is more than probable that the band of the Munsters will come up from Dum Dum for a few months and that if sufficient support is not voluntarily offered it, a small charge will be made, as at home and everywhere, for the seats on the Chowrusta.

A crashing thunderstorm, followed by heavy and continuous rain burst over the station on Sunday night and today it is so wet that if not too soon for the monsoon I should be inclined to say that the rains had set in. They do not, however, begin earlier here than the middle of June. Over 2 inches of rain fell and was much wanted after the dry weather and heat of the last two weeks for the tea and all cultivation.

The Bretheren of the Masonic Lodge are growing in numbers every-day, in short it is now fashionable to be a mason. The large gathering the other evening had over 43 members present and Mr. R. I. Harrison of Lebong was elected Master for the ensuing year in succession to Worshipful Past Master Ronald Bateman.

Major Webb after a service of 30 years retires from the Command of the Darjeeling Troop of Volunteers and will probably be succeeded by Lieutenant Grant Gordon.

Our Amateur Dramatic Club has the well known comedy Betsina in rehearsal to be performed in Jubilee Week and as the cast is a strong one and the piece very amusing a pleasant evening is expected.

Darjeeling - from our correspondent - June 9th 1897.

A young lady who is up here for the season, had her piano packed to be bought up here, before leaving her home below about three months ago. It arrived the other day and on being opened a young cobra about two feet long and thick as a finger wriggled out from the straw. It was killed before it could do any harm and the owner of the piano was trying to think out how the snake got into the case and how it survived for three months with nothing but straw to live on. Snakes, as we know, love music but it is doubtful that they can live for months on the mere memory of it.

The last tie of the Billiard Handicap between Barnard and Allan was played last Saturday...

June 15th 1897 - *Friend of India* by telegraph from various correspondents.

Darjeeling was shaken at 5 o'clock yesterday evening by the most appalling earthquake. The severest ever known here. The shock lasted three minutes and has done incalculable damage. Every house in the place has been more or less affected. Those who have suffered most severely are the Maharaja of Burdwan's property at Rose Bank, Mr. Castle's house, Singamari....

As the weather is very peculiar there are fears of another shock in which case the loss of property would probably be terrible. So far I have not heard of any loss of life. For fifteen minutes after the earthquake there was a distinct rumbling sound and a peculiar stillness and oppressiveness of the atmosphere which seemed to forbode evil and as expected there were no less than four shocks from 11 to 4 last night, another at 9 this morning, and another at noon and another at 5 this evening. Fortunately they were slight shocks which apparently caused no further damage. It has been raining off and on since noon and the general opinion is that we are not safe yet...

The earthquake came within the higher isoseismals of the Assam Earthquake of the 12th June 1897. The next severe earthquake in this area was the Bihar-Nepal Earthquake of the 15th January 1934.

14

Rain And More Rain

At the end of every June, when the monsoon is due to break, the giants have their annual general meeting. There is much disagreement and the meetings are stormy. Sparks flash like lightning and thunderous roars reverberate through the mountains and valleys. There is always much unfinished business from their meetings which is left to work itself out in grumbles, irritations and fights which will continue intermittently until the Festival of Light, the Hindu Diwali at the beginning of the fine weather causes the giants to put aside their grumbles and enjoy the sunny days.

The pictorial setting for these storms is a landscape of up to 100 miles in depth, a distance one can on a clear day see from Darjeeling's Tiger Hill to Mount Everest, the distance, say, from London to the Wash. The mountains, Everest and Kanchenjunga and all the lesser peaks form the background against which the lightning flashes. The valleys, thousands of feet deep, give resonance to the thunder.

Storms were a regular feature of Darjeeling life and of the weather patterns. Some, of course, were worse than others. A major storm which the British in Darjeeling were to experience was a cyclone on September 1899. Of this storm, Arthur Dash, writing in the *Darjeeling Gazetteer* of 1945 has this to say:

> Although normally wind force is small in all parts of the District, storms occur from time to time accompanied by heavy rainfall and winds of great force. Such a storm took place in September 1899. 19-40 inches (depending on exact location) of rain fell at Darjeeling (the maximum fall during 24 hours recorded during 48 years). This followed heavy rainfalls on the 23 and 24 September these coming after an already heavy seasonal rainfall caused many disastrous landslips, loss of life and destruction of houses, roads and property. The storm originated in a disturbance coming from the Bay of Bengal and the centre passed through the western part of the District close to Darjeeling and Pulbazar. Rainfall was much less heavy at Kalimpong and at Pedong only 7.58 inches were recorded. On the other hand 27.20 inches fell in the Happy Valley Tea Estate near Darjeeling and at Pulbazar the little Rangit rose from 30 to 50 feet and 67 deaths resulted. This flood was due to landslips upstream damming up water: when these dams burst, huge masses of water were projected into the river bed and caused an abnormal rise in river-level.

The Tista came down in a flood of unprecedented height and most of the houses in the Tista Bazar and whole sections of the Tista valley road disappeared. (This was the road along which the Derbyshires had marched.) Two thousand acres of tea and large stretches of forest were swept away; the most serious forest damage being in the Balasan river valley where three-quarters of the Balasan forest was destroyed. Very great damage was done to road and rail communications in the district and the stoppage of transport caused distress and soaring prices. The total loss of life in the district was 219 and in Darjeeling town 72 were killed (including 10 Europeans). Along the eastern side of the Mall was an almost continuous series of landslides.

Immediately after the disaster, a Committee of engineers and residents was appointed to devise measures to prevent recurrence of landslips or to minimise their consequences. The report of the Committee, which was assisted by a member of the Geological Survey, showed that the slips were confined to the soil-cap and that the under-lying rock was massive and secure. The report clearly traced the cause of each slip and indicated the remedial measures needed. These required legislation and the result has been special drainage and building regulations applicable to hill municipalities and adequate powers to ensure properly designed buildings, drain, roads and protective sloping of hillsides on private and public land. With these powers the authorities have succeeded in preventing slips occurring subsequently under similar conditions.

Across the valley of the Rangit from Singla and Tukvar can be seen a great and horrible scar where a landslip tore through the covering forest, and the steepness of the mountain side is such that insufficient soil was left for the regrowth of vegetation. The scar remains as a reminder of the violence of nature.

The Englishman reported that:

Among the deeds of heroism worthy of mention is the rescue work done by the boys of St. Joseph's College. A village settlement was swept away on the Lebong road. The boys dug out seven dead and succeeded in rescuing two men who were still alive. One woman was pinned between two trees; the boys rescued her alive and carried her on their shoulders to the hospital.

In Darjeeling the damage from the storm was repaired and the students of St. Michael's School for girls, the Anglican foundation, were given a new site for their school. It was not too difficult to tidy away the damage to buildings, but that scar on the Sikkim hillside remains as a reminder to all who come to admire the Darjeeling scenery and to dance the night away in the balls, that outside there is a weather pattern in these beautiful hills, and that weather is controlled by some giant living in his mountain hideaway.

The Annual Report for the Soom Tea estate for 1899 refers to the storms and their effect on a promising year:

The quality of the produce showed an improvement last season and we trust this will be maintained. The Manager (Mr. G. Nash) finds it necessary to estimate for a smaller crop than last year, in consequence of the damage done to the Gardens by the Cyclone in September last. Had it not been for the loss of plucking area caused by the storm and cloud burst on 25 September, and for the cold weather which immediately followed, the crop would have been nearer 1,700 maunds. Work of uncovering bushes buried under landslips was taken in hand after the storm and close on 96,000 bushes in 30 acres have been recovered. Another 15 to 20 acres of slips may be replanted.

The Manager of Tukvar, Mr. FA Möller, records:
Heavy rain which accompanied the cyclone of 25th of that month apparently chilled the soil as the bushes did not flush at all freely after that date. At Singla a 20 acre block of nice land has been cleared, in lieu of the part of the Singla flat which was destroyed by the Rungnit river.

As was said earlier, damage by slips was an ongoing problem. Nash, the Soom Manager wrote in January 1903:
The heavy rain in September caused almost as much damage as the Cyclone of 1899. The rain registered on 25th and 26th was over 15 inches. The area of tea actually lost at the time was more than about 3 acres but a large block of land, with 10 - 12 acres of tea has broken up and subsided, and shows huge cracks and fissures. This land is bound to go in blocks at a later time.

Eva, the author's mother, was at Tukvar in September 1950 when there was another disaster. The following is a personal account of such an experience on a tea estate.
Monsoon conditions are getting in under the influence of a depression in the North Bay, which this morning, Friday, was centred about 300 miles South east of Calcutta. Thus the Alipore Meteorologists recorded the advent of the monsoon.

On the same day in Darjeeling Dr. Katju, Governor of West Bengal, was entertained by the Mahrattas to a display of PT, followed by tea on the terrace of the Officers' Mess and the playing of The Retreat by the Mahratta Band. Although on the previous evening there had been as much as four inches of rain in Darjeeling there was nothing to suggest that it was other than a normal breaking of the monsoon, and on Saturday, the 10th June, quite a number of the usual Saturday visitors to Darjeeling came in for meetings and to attend the last day of the Races. There was a slight drizzle and when the planters applauded it as an end to the prolonged drought which had seriously affected their crop, the shop keepers grumbled that such rain "might be good for crops, but it was bad for humans."

By Saturday evening many roads leading to the tea estates were becoming difficult for motor traffic. From Saturday at dusk, rain, unremitting and relentless, left no doubt that the monsoon was on us.

On Sunday morning we here measured 7.91 inches, but still the rain went on, and satisfaction in the planters' minds turned to a slight uneasiness. Still, an urgent conference encouraged 'Himself' to brave the journey to Darjeeling, a matter of five miles by jeep, which was, in fact, with the help of men to give the occasional push, safely accomplished.

But a telephone call put through after lunch told of disasters in Darjeeling. Many of the coolie houses, perched on stilts on the hillsides outside the town, or crowded together in huddled confusion below the bazaar were either slipping down the slopes or were in danger. Even larger concrete buildings were moving in the town itself, and in a panic one tried to imagine just how human agency could deal with the situation. Then came reports of deaths and casualties, bodies that could not be traced as the hillsides became an avalanche of mud.

Electric pylons were carried away, and the town and nearby district was left without light or electric power. The telephone service next succumbed, posts, wires, all in an inextricable mass. And still the rain beat down upon the corrugated iron roofs with deafening insistence, if there was a slight lull for a moment one heard the roar of the rivers, 4,000 feet and six miles below, increasing in volume and terrifying power as the day wore on.

By 4 p.m. a further 4.70 inches had been measured and an hour later with what relief we welcomed 'Himself'. The jeep had been abandoned, and he had walked the last three miles of what had once been the main road which leads down to the river and to the boundary of Sikkim.

Half an hour earlier a distracted chowkidar had arrived from the upper division with a tale of woe, part of a concrete revetment had become dislodged, hurtled down into a coolie house and killed a one year old child.

In an attempt to make the best of a bad job we settled to listen to the wireless, a symphony concert, Beethoven's Emperor Concerto, but with the first strains, out went the lights and off went the current, tapped from the Darjeeling supply. A mad scramble to find at least one candle and a torch.

A restless night, filled with the roar of rain and river, and occasionally - was it? - yet another landslide? From which direction this time?

Next morning early astir. The occasional click click of a daring cricket and a faint chirrup from some bolder bird. For five minutes the rain stopped and we dared to hope. The vegetable garden didn't look too bad, although another 4.98 inches were recorded. The rows and rows of gladioli, though a little dashed, were still upright, even the vegetables were not beaten down, though baby carrots had been washed out of the ground and the newly-planted runner beans were on top of their beds holding up rather pathetic shoots. But skilful fingers soon tucked them in again. At 7 a.m. went the gong for work, for plucking the tea which now showed so much promise after the rain. But again the deluge, as unrelenting as ever.

And what a day was heralded! A day of terror for poor wretched people in houses quite inadequate to withstand an onslaught such as this. Just below our bungalow the whole hillside began to move, a slip at first 50 feet wide extended its length down through newly-planted forest, through well-established tea, to a village of lines below. But worse was to come. The end house of a row was swept away. A falling beam killed an old woman, mother of our head contractor, the house from which the beam fell took with it a nurse, her small son and daughter. The father of this family extracted himself from that river of liquid mud, but no trace was found of the others.

How could one deal with mud in drenching rain, when as fast as a tool made a gap that gap was filled again? After two hours of frenzied digging the body of the nurse was recovered. By noon the girl's body also was found, but only four days later did the boy's body come to light. A goat with a broken leg, a cat also survived from that house, and the one flicker of light relief was provided by the discovery of a hen, safely cushioned under a beam, who had occupied her waiting hours by laying an egg. Such is Nature's urge for survival!

By Monday evening many other houses had already slipped or were threatening to do so, and it became imperative before nightfall to arrange evacuation for many homeless families. But how to keep check of over 1700 acres?

They camped out in the school, in parts of the factory, in the assistant's vacant bungalows, with other more fortunate friends. Arrangements had to be made for food and cooking, and what was to be done with the precious cow or goat? The house of the Head Clerk showed a crack a foot wide and had to be abandoned. Under the office of 'Himself' the ground slipped away and files and documents must be rescued, worse a bank behind a new concrete store house where is housed the precious rice stocks came down, and the water rose to door level before frantic digging directed the rushing mud into, we hoped, safer channels.

Through the gaps of moving clouds enormous slips at the concrete bases of the pylons sustaining the ropeway on which the estate depends for its despatch and receipt of stores added to the unbearable anxiety. We knew already that our motor road to Darjeeling had gone.

Despondency, deep and unshakeable, was the only response from the labour. 'What can one do?' was their only reply The inevitability of that rain, and more, of that moving mud, was horrible. By midnight we again dared to hope. Surely the rain was a little less heavy drumming on the roof... Yes, we could hear the rushing torrents of the great water sources now. And what a roaring! But indeed, we could now hope that there was a slackening and the morning rain gauge measurement of 1.42 inches re-assured us.

As the clouds drifted on every side it looked as though an angry giant, with savage fearsome nails, had lashed out in fury, scouring long red clefts where before the hillsides had been covered green with forest and tea.

Still the far-away rivers roared. Reports came in of villages, bazaars and bridges being swept away in the torrents, which bore down a swirling mass of trees and wreckage. Men of the baser sort risked their lives to loot such goods as they could, rolls of cloth, cases of stores as they were carried rushing down.

That year the weather was exceptionally bad, but storms, landslips, broken communications are a regular feature of the monsoon and the weather pattern, as autumn colours and winter frosts are in Britain, and one just got on with the business of living and tried to ignore the weather except that if one was sensible, one arranged to do as little travelling as possible during the monsoons.

Throughout the rains I spent in Kalimpong in 1955 I was fortunate enough, and travelled regularly backwards and forwards to Darjeeling with little to no excitement, other than that normally occasioned by the daily Landrover service. I had learnt to ignore the fact that the driver always switched the engine off to coast down the steep hills to save petrol! Improvement in the road engineering ensured that severe landslides were not frequent and the smaller slips were often negotiable. It was worse on the narrow, twisty, dirt roads of the tea estates. As I wrote:

We left the party eventually at about 1.30 a.m. and the road was like a skating rink and we skidded all the way up. When we eventually came to the slip, it wasn't a very big one, fortunately and the road was just covered, about two feet high with soft wet mud. Eric put the car into bottom gear and charged it. I was most surprised when we came out the other side intact... But, later, on our road down to Tukvar there was another small slip and we had to move a boulder out of the way, and just managed to wriggle the narrow jeep round a tree trunk but the Tuffnals coming down behind us in their car had to move the trunk right aside before their wider car could pass.

The Tukvar road is classified as a District Board road through to the Sikkim border and this rough, stony track is famous for its hair-pin bends. The most famous of these is called the 'cobbled gumpti'. No vehicle could negotiate this corner without reversing at least once, often twice. The gradient at this point being 1 in 3. In an attempt to make the corner easier, concrete tracks had been laid and, to widen the corner itself, a wooden parapet, a flimsy structure, had been built out over a ravine. I was travelling up this road one day with my elderly godfather, and my father's predecessor as Manager of Tukvar, when he ran into trouble. At the side of the road here was a horse trough, this was not only to refresh the ponies - in the days before the ropeway was built, all the tea chests were carried up the hill by pack ponies - after their long haul up the steep slope, but was used to refill the car radiators. On this particular occasion the men, working on the corner had decided that their work on the road would look better if they washed the concrete down. The result was a mixture of slippery slurry on the concrete which made it impossible for the wheels to grip once the car had lost momentum. So having begun to negotiate the corner the car was left with its back to the ravine. I was commanded out of the car and then, for what seemed like an age, the car, with my godfather at the wheel, slid nearer and nearer to the edge, then, at the last minute the men who had been working on the road were able to stop it. There was always a supply of large stones at the side of these corners, it was one of these rocks which had, eventually, arrested the slide.

My mother would always comment that it was 'the wife' who had to get out and put the stone under the wheel on these corners, no matter how wet or muddy the road. There was one bachelor who perfected a technique for throwing a stone behind his back wheel while he sat in the driver's seat. A stone, secured to a rope was kept in the car for this purpose.

After one particularly slippery drive down to Tukvar in the jeep, I wrote that one could tell when the driver had the brake on because the wheels had ceased to go round!

The road to Tukvar (1954)

15

The Road to Lhasa and Everest

The last chapter strayed too far into the twentieth century and we must go back in time to the end of the 19th and the early years of the 20th century.

Sister Gabriel, the last surviving person to see Darjeeling grow from a few shacks into a Victorian town, died in January 1905. She was one of the first Loreto nuns to come to Darjeeling in 1846. As their housekeeper she had learnt to manage. As cook and housekeeper she had lived through the days when it was not even possible to make bread because no flour was available, a situation improved when the fateful garrison at Katapaha was opened. She had seen Darjeeling grow and with her never failing sense of humour had supported her fellow nuns through those most trying years. In 1904 she remained a link with the pioneer age.

While Darjeeling danced its way into the world's social calendar, relations between Britain and Tibet deteriorated from border skirmishes and petty kidnappings into the harsh world of 20th century power politics.

The Tsarist Empire was advancing eastwards and Lord Curzon, the new Viceroy of India, was almost pathological in his fear of the Russians. A Chinese man, Kang-yu-Wai, living in Darjeeling, added the catalyst to these fears when he wrote a letter to the effect that China was about to hand over Tibet to Russia, allowing it to build a fort and railways. These rumours, substantiated from other sources, were taken seriously.

After the Derbyshires had thrown the Tibetans back across the Nathu La pass in 1888, an agreement between China and Britain, and another between Sikkim, Tibet and Britain, delineated the Sikkim frontier and confirmed that Sikkim was a British protectorate. This agreement also accepted that Tibet remained under Peking's control. The Tibetans, on the other hand, not only ignored the existence of the treaty but did what they could to sabotage it. When Lord Curzon wrote politely to the Dalai Lama in Lhasa, his letter, having been delivered, was returned unopened. Lord Curzon tried again, but this time the letter, again returned, is reported not to have been delivered as the messenger was frightened for his life. British Imperialism was being challenged by a nonentity.

War was still not considered to be immediate. Lord Curzon sent the explorer Francis Younghusband to talk with the Tibetans. Younghusband seemed the obvious man for such a delicate job. He had received the Royal Geographical Society's Gold Medal in 1889 for his explorations in Central Asia, he was also a trained soldier and skilled negotiator, with a particular interest in Tibet. With him went Claude White - who had returned to Sikkim from Darjeeling after his spell of convalescing - and who was the Political Officer for Sikkim, and together with two hundred Indian troops they left Kalimpong for the Tibetan border. The Tibetans refused to negotiate; they would only negotiate on the British side of the border and they were not prepared to cross the border for that purpose. It is a story with a familiar ring to it!

It became too much for Lord Curzon who was not prepared to allow the Tibetans to think that they had won a victory because they had mistaken forbearance for weakness. London responded immediately to Curzon's request to send troops into Tibet and Francis Younghusand, promoted to Colonel, was ordered to obtain satisfaction. It was to be a punitive expedition, nothing else. Francis Younghusband was appointed as Political Officer, and with him went Brigadier General Macdonald and an army of over 1,000 soldiers. Instructions were vague, neither man was given over all command.

The season in Darjeeling was over, the summer visitors had gone and with the view of the Snowy Mountains at its best, preparations for the Tibet invasion went ahead. In the winter of 1903 Francis Younghusband left his wife in Darjeeling and marshalling his forces, he left Kalimpong early one morning.

It was mid winter when a mounted soldier bearing the Union Jack crossed the snow covered Jelep La into Tibet. Behind him struggled 10,000 coolies, 7,000 mules, 4,000 yaks, six camels and correspondents from *The Times*, the *Daily Mail,* and Reuters.

This force was led by either General Macdonald or Francis Younghusband and the lack of clarity in the leadership did nothing to simplify either the expedition or the outcome. It was a tragic business, made worse by the confusion over who was actually in total command. Although turkey and plum puddings were sent from Darjeeling for the Christmas celebrations, the conditions under which the expedition worked were appalling. The British were transporting guns and ammunition into a country protected by giant mountains and cruel weather, to face a foe armed with courage, tenacity, religious fervour and the weapons of the Middle Ages.

Edmund Candler, the *Daily Mail* correspondent wrote 'A driving hurricane made it impossible to light a fire or cook food. The officers were reduced to frozen bully beef and neat spirits, while the sepoys went without food for thirty-six hours... The drivers arrived at Tuna frozen to the waist. Twenty men of the 12th Mule Corps were frostbitten, and thirty men of the 23rd Pioneers were so incapacitated that they had to be carried in on mules. On the same day there were seventy cases of snow-blindness among the 8th Gurkhas.'

Again Candler wrote 'The great difficulties we experienced in pushing through supplies to Tuna, which is less than 150 miles from Siliguri, show the absurdity of the idea of a Russian advance on Lhasa. The nearest Russian outpost is over 1,000 miles distant, and the country to be traversed is even more barren and inhospitable than on our frontier.'

In spite of hardships and difficulties the army pushed on. The first fighting was at Guru. The first casualty was Candler who had his hand slashed off by a Tibetan sword, by one of the Tibetans who were resisting an attempt to disarm them.

The rest was a massacre. The records suggest that between 500 and 700 Tibetans were slaughtered. Candler said 'The impossible had happened. Prayers and charms and mantras, and the holiest of their holy men, had failed them.' But the courage, the religious fanaticism and the determination of that courageous people was not dimmed. Before the year was out, many more Tibetans were killed. Why? - they refused to talk to the British on Tibetan soil. They would only talk across the border.

The British army went on. The battle for the Karo Pass made military history - at 16,000 feet it was the highest battle ever fought by the British, probably by anyone, and it was probably only due to their superiority of fire power that the British were able to take it. The Tibetans continued with their refusal to negotiate.

They talked in Lhasa. And while they talked, the British army's medical team did what it could to help the enemy wounded. Then the storm broke, the world was offended.

On the 22nd October 1903 the *Army and Navy Gazette* reported:
Considerations which arise out of the Tibetan Expedition are from several points of view of the utmost seriousness. The religious feelings of a large part of our native army have been offended and perhaps 50,000 native soldiers, including the reserves consider that we had no justification of intruding into the great sanctuary of Buddhism. It is impossible to calculate what the effect may ultimately be on the native army, certainly the expedition will be discussed with disapprobation in every village of our Buddhist population and throughout Nepal and Bhutan.

The Anglo Tibetan Convention was finally signed in Lhasa, and was a personal triumph for Francis Younghusband's powers of persuasion. It was a bizarre affair. The Treaty signed, the army free to leave was given as noisy a farewell as they had a welcome! The very Tibetans who had fought hard to keep the British out were full of tumultuous demonstrations of goodwill for their new friends.

It is to Candler of the *Daily Mail* that we must look to for the post script when all was over and three Tibetans were released from the Lhasa state dungeons where they had been placed for assisting Chandra Das and the Japanese Ekai Kawaguchi:

105

An old man and his son were brought into the hall looking utterly bowed and broken. The old man's chains had been removed from his limbs that morning for the first time in twenty years, and he came in blinking at the unaccustomed light like a blind man miraculously restored to sight. His offence was hospitality shown to Chandra Das in 1884. An old monk of Sera was released next. His offence had been that he had been the teacher of Kawaguchi, the Japanese traveller who visited Lhasa in the guise of a Chinese pilgrim. We who looked on these sad relics of humanity felt that their restitution to liberty was in itself sufficient to justify our advance on Lhasa. (Kawaguchi also set up house for a while in Darjeeling.)

The British Army left Lhasa on 23rd September 1904, seven weeks after entering the capital. Others, however, had left before, men like Perceval Landon who left as soon as he had collected all the material he needed to rush out his account of the battle with the Tibetans for Lhasa. Landon is reported to have covered the 400 miles from Lhasa to the nearest railhead, Darjeeling, in eleven days, travelling on horseback. It took him thirty-five days to reach London, a considerable achievement. Just four months after he had left Lhasa his two volume work was in the London bookshops. It was a journalistic coup!

Tibet however was not to be an open country, it was still to retain its mystique for Younghusband understood and appreciated the Tibetans. The British wanted no further trouble with Tibet and the one way of ensuring this, was to keep the frontier closed. This policy enabled friendships, particularly that with the Dalai Lama, to flourish and trade to benefit. It is not within the scope of these pages to discuss what should or should not have been done in Tibet, merely to make a reference from time to time because of the involvement of those living in Darjeeling, with Tibetan affairs.

To develop trade, some agents were allowed into Tibet. One such agent was David Macdonald, the Trade Agent at Shigatse. He married a Tibetan, and when he retired, he settled in Kalimpong where he and his family ran the Himalayan Hotel. It was from this address that Macdonald kept in contact with Lhasa and the thirteenth Dalai Lama, Thupten Gyatso, and it was he who continued to keep Sir Charles Bell, who had also retired from Tibet, informed of the problems when the Dalai Lama died.

When I stayed at the Himalayan Hotel in 1954 I found that I had stepped into a different world. The hotel was run by David Macdonald's daughters wearing Tibetan dress, those cleverly woven striped aprons, which the women wore over their long skirts under which the embroidered boots, often red, can be seen. The living room of the hotel was adorned with the prayer pictures, the Tibetan tankhas, and Tibetan rugs lay on the floors and were also strewn over the sofas. These gay rugs often depict fearsome dragons in bright vivid colours, orange and reds on a dark background.

Kenneth Graham Homes, Kalimpong; church, school and clock tower (1954)

It was winter time when I was there, the nights were cold and to warm the room a sigri, a bright blazing charcoal brazier was brought in and placed in the centre of the room. My letters express utter astonishment at the efficiency of this heating system. There was no unpleasant smoke from the glowing charcoal and placed in the middle of the room, the heat was able to reach outwards to warm everyone.

Yet again we have gone too far forward in time and must return to the events which followed on after this new peace.

Now that the Tibetan frontier had been crossed and there had been dialogue with the Tibetans, mountaineers could look hopefully at Peak XV, Mount Everest and hope that soon Europeans would be able to walk on its slopes and possibly even attempt to climb it. Ever since the mountain was discovered to be the highest one in the world, men had dreamt of standing on its summit. Two of the Indian explorers, one of whom was Chandra Das, were the only foreigners in Tibet known to have travelled in the Everest region, but they were not mountaineers and Chandra Das's account, although it told of the hardships of travelling in such country, was vague and uninformative.

When the British moved out of Lhasa in 1904, Captain Rawling and Major Ryder went on a detour and surveyed the Tsampo Valley and the mountains round about. Unfortunately winter was approaching and they were unable to reconnoitre the northern approaches to Mount Everest, but it was a beginning. Captain John Noel in his book 'The Story of Everest' wrote:

107

As late therefore as the early years of the present century, the journey of Sarat Chandra Das, who passed by the east, and the journey of the Explorer 'M.H' who passed by the west, comprised the sum total of our knowledge of the approaches to Mount Everest... No explorer had penetrated to Everest's glacier valleys. The area surrounding the great summit, which had been plotted by the observation from India, was a blank white space on the map. The mountain stood, stupendous, seen through telescopes: its slope untrodden by human beings as far as we know.

The first European to get within forty miles of Everest's base was Captain Noel in 1913 and then he was travelling in disguise through Tibet.

Finally, after the Great War, the British Envoy to Lhasa, Sir Charles Bell, obtained permission of the Tibetan Government for two exploratory and climbing parties to approach Everest, in 1921 and 1922. The 1921 reconnaissance expedition was led by Lt. Col. Howard-Bury and Dr. Kellas. The youngest man of this expedition was George Leigh-Mallory. The expedition, like all the pre-1940 expeditions, assembled in Darjeeling, before making its way down the ridge to Pashoke, across the Teesta and up to Kalimpong. These expeditions paused at Pashoke, and in the bungalow of Pashoke Tea Estate I was able to see the signatures of all the early Everest climbers. It was a solid, old wall on which they had all measured their heights and signed their names including that of George Herbert Leigh-Mallory on his last fateful trip.

In 1948 James Ramsey Ullman wrote of the man who was to die on, or near, the summit of Everest in 1924:

Mallory remains, almost a quarter of a century after his death, the most famous and probably the greatest, of Everest climbers...

Everest was George Mallory's mountain, more than any other man's. He had pioneered the way to it and blazed the trail to its heights; his flaming spirit had been the principal driving force behind each attack; the conquest of the summit was the great dream of his life. His companions, watching him during these early June days of 1924, realised that he was preparing for his mightiest effort.

And right from the start, the men that helped make the expeditions possible were the Sherpa porters. Before the first expeditions had even left for the mountain, Dr. AM Kellas, who lived a double life of London research chemist and explorer-mountaineer, trained a corps of Sherpa guides and porters. Tenzing, the Sherpa, who with Edmund Hillary, was the first man to reach the summit of Everest and return, says in his autobiography:

It is strange about the name Sherpa. The world hears it only in connection with mountains and expeditions, and many people think it is a word meaning 'porter' or 'guide'. But this is not so at all. The Sherpas are a people, a tribe. According to those who have studied such things, there are about a hundred thousand of us, dwellers in the high uplands of the Eastern Himalayas...

My dreams were of Lhasa when I was very young. Later I began to hear and think about other places. For many years Sherpas had gone from Solo Khumbu across the mountains and forests to Darjeeling, to work on the tea plantations or as porters and rickshaw coolies, and sometimes they would come back and tell about it. Then something even more interesting began to happen. An Englishman, called Dr. Kellas, who was a noted explorer and climber, hired Sherpas from Darjeeling to go out with him into the mountains; a little later General Bruce, of the Indian Army, also took some on his expeditions; and soon that was what most of the Darjeeling sherpas were doing - working as porters and helpers on expeditions to the high Himalayas. Although I did not know it at the time, it was then that our people began to earn their reputation as the best of all mountain men, which we have kept with pride ever since...

...I knew that I could not stay in Solo Khumbu for ever - that I was not made to be a farmer or a herder - and late in 1932, when I was eighteen, I left home again, this time not for Kathmandu but Darjeeling, and though once more I seemed to be turning my back on Chomolungma (Everest), I felt that really I was going towards it; for now the word had spread that there was to be another expedition in 1933 and I was determined to go with it if I possibly could.

There were twelve of us who left home together - both boys and girls and we had been planning it for a month, holding secret meetings and collecting food and supplies...

One of my companions was Dawa Thondup, who has since become a famous Sherpa. He was older than I, and though he had never been to Darjeeling, he seemed to know a lot about it, talking about the next expedition that would soon be leaving for Everest, and how we would surely get jobs with it.

At first I did not stay in Darjeeling, but in a near-by village called Alubari, which means 'place where potatoes grow'. It was Ringa Lama who took me there, and he arranged that I should live with a cousin of his who was named Pouri. Pouri had fifteen cows, and it was my job to take care of them and also to do general work about the place. Here I began to learn the Nepali language, which is much used in Darjeeling, and also Yalmo, another speech of the region. My best teacher was a man called Manbahadur Tamang, who worked with me cutting grass for the cows, and I was very grateful to him. To-day Tamang and I are old friends, and recently he has been working for me as a mason on my new house (in Darjeeling). Often we talk of those early days, remembering this and that - and especially how one day, when we were gathering firewood in a restricted area, a forest guard came along, tied us to a tree, and beat us.

Sometimes, when I was working for Pouri, I was sent into Darjeeling to sell milk. And these were great days for me, because that was where I wanted to be. The town is built on the side of a steep hill, looking north, and about fifty miles away, across the deep valleys of Sikkim, is the main eastern range of the Himalayas, with Kangehenjunga [alternative spelling to Kanchenjunga] in the centre. Often I used to look at it, standing great and white in the sky, and this would make me feel good, because I knew then that even in this strange new world, I was not too far away from the mountains that I loved. Then too, here was Darjeeling itself, and this was a marvellous place to a young boy from the country. At the bottom of the big hill was the old part of the town, with its bazaars and temples and narrow, crowded streets, which reminded me somewhat of Kathmandu. But higher up, in the strange part, everything was different and new. Here were the homes of the English and richer Indians; fine stores and tea-house and a moving-picture theatre; Government House, a maharaja's palace, and a hotel like a castle. I am afraid I paid much less attention to my cans of milk than to all these wonders that lay around me.

...Back in Darjeeling, I did not return to Alubari, with its cows and potatoes, but moved into the town itself. There were two districts where most of the Sherpas lived, called Toong Soong Busti and Bhutia Busti (busti means village), and I stayed in Toong Soong, which has been my home for much of the time ever since. By good luck I became a tenant in the house of Angtharkay, who was already an experienced mountaineer, and to-day ranks as one of the most celebrated of all Sherpas. And soon I was no longer the lonely outsider I had been before. Near by lived my old friend Dawa Thondup, now also a veteran, and all round were other men who had won fame on Everest and elsewhere.

Tenzing's success and the whole success of Lord Hunt's Everest expedition which culminated in their joint conquest of the mountain, laid the foundations for the sport of mountaineering in India. I was in Darjeeling 4th November 1954 and managed to get an invitation to see Pandit Nehru lay the foundation stone of the Mountaineering School. A suitable rock for training purposes had

The 'training' rock on the Lebong road (Tenzing?)

been found just off the Lebong road, Darjeeling and the large house, which during the war had been empty and which we, at school referred to as 'the haunted house', was the first centre. It was here, that, as my letters record:

At 9 o'clock he (Nehru) laid the stone to the mountaineering School, about three miles away from the school and the rock! We then walked down to the rock. The Governor remarked to my father, that when he went for his walk in the morning he saw the mountaineers climbing all over it roped together. In the afternoon he goes by to see the small school boys playing on it!

After Nehru had laid the stone, which incidentally got stuck and didn't lay, he had made his speech in Hindi, we speak Nepalese here!!! Then we went down to the rock and saw an opening demonstration. This I must say was quite impressive and very interesting and I got so excited taking snaps that I forgot to turn the film on!!! After that we went to Rungnit T.E. for lunch then Mop and Pop went to the Shrubbery (Government House) to hear Nehru speak in Urdu this time!! Then they went on to have tea but I wasn't invited there.

It was this occasion that first introduced me to the greatness of the Sherpas who, before that demonstration, I had thought, in my ignorance, were only porters and not skilled mountaineers and this, in spite of the fact that I knew all about Tenzing's achievements, I had considered him to be just the exception to

111

the rule. Since that time I have learnt to have a great respect for them and their achievements.

It was to Angtharkay's house that I was taken when preparing to go into the Sikkim hills. We were an assorted group of four who had got together because individually we all wished to trek into Sikkim and needed companions. Because I had the right contacts it was I who had to make all the arrangements, for passes, porters and dak bungalows. But once I had met Angtharkay all my worries, except the passes, were at an end. He was efficiency itself, took control and made all the arrangements for the Sherpas and told me what was required. It was he who arranged for Tenzing's friend, Thondup, to be our cook/Sirdar, in charge of our six Sherpas. He had been cook with the New Zealand Expedition in 1951 and had been up on Cho Oyu in 1952 and then with Sir John Hunt on the famous Everest Expedition in 1953 (when Hillary and Tenzing reached the summit); he had been the head cook and went up as far as Camp IV. According to custom Thondup would carry no loads but do the cooking and take charge of the trip.

With such distinguished mountain men my trip into the Sikkim hills can be described as no more than a little 'stroll'. One of the most outstanding things of this little 'stroll' of mine was that of companionships, not only with my fellow trekkers whom I had hardly known before we began, but the companionship we also shared with the porters. One had recently returned from the successful Kanchenjunga Expedition and was at great pains to explain that he hadn't been on Everest because he had gone off on another expedition to somewhere, I've forgotten the name, and then reeled off a list of other great mountains he had been on. For the first part of the trip he wore a bright red jumper. We called him 'fancy pants' as he took great pride in his appearance and unlike the other porters and ourselves was always washing his clothes. Then there were two young boys who were great fun and who, as they put it, 'were learning the trade'. On the last stage of our journey the youngest one fell in with a group of people who told him that his father had died six days ago. Poor chap, he was very upset and so were we all as by that time, we felt like one family.

16

Tomato Ketchup

Today the thought of dressing for dinner in the jungle is ridiculous but the Victorian etiquette of the 19th century set the seal on tea garden life until the Second World War. The arrival of the motor car in the hill districts during the end of the 1920s made some significant difference in that one could drive out with something approaching the required dignity. But as many a wife can testify, 'dignity' is lost when the car failed to negotiate a corner and it was she, in long dinner dress who had to leap out into the mud and rain, find, and then place, a rock behind the wheel. That rock often being all there was between the car, her husband and death at the bottom of some ravine. Although my parents, Eva and Malcolm Betten, did not go out to tea until the first quarter of the 20th century was past, their experience spans the Victorian and post Second World War life styles.

Malcolm was appointed to Nagri Farm by the firm of George Williamson which he had joined in 1925, having completed his engineering training at Petters in Yeovil. Nagri Farm, which had been incorporated as a tea company in 1901, tried also to be a farm. In fact it was the original intention that the farming side of the enterprise should continue but the effort put into the keeping of the dairy cows and poultry was always half hearted. Nagri Farm Tea Estate was fifteen miles from the nearest earth road which again was twenty miles from the nearest town, Darjeeling. However, it should be remembered that real distance in the mountains is not measured in miles travelled, but rather in time and effort expended.

When Malcom arrived at Nagri Farm on New Year's Eve he had been travelling for weeks. First there had been the sea trip from England to Calcutta; from Calcutta there was the overnight express train to Siliguri where he changed onto the Darjeeling Himalayan Railway, the DHR, to experience the thrills of climbing into the mountains, passed Sensation Corner and Agony Point. The next thirty odd miles took over four hours as the little train puffed and puffed up the hillside with a boy sitting on the front bumper sprinkling sand on the rails in an effort to prevent wheelspin. At Kurseong, the train stopped in the main street, which also served as the station, before puffing off to Sonada. Malcolm left the train at Sonada, the spot Colonel Lloyd had called Senen Dah, the bear's den. Here a pony and some porters for his luggage, were waiting for him.

Leaving his luggage with the porters he rode off on the last leg of his journey. No one had advised him that since this was not only New Year's Eve but evening time, he should arrive at his manager's bungalow ready and correctly dressed for dinner!

In the first five minutes of his arrival at Nagri Farm, Malcolm learnt that assistants 'are the lowest form of human life'. Without correct clothes he could not join in the festivities with the few neighbours who had gathered at his manager's bungalow.

Malcolm now had to experience several lonely years in a small, isolated bungalow, learning the language and all about tea. Fortunately for Malcolm, George Williamson's were more humane than some agencies because they did permit their assistants to marry. However, they had no control over the manner in which the managers treated their assistants, and obviously, as Eva found, some managers and their wives were better and kinder than others. After only a couple of years, Malcolm was able to bring his bride, Eva, to Nagri Farm. They were married in Calcutta, more or less straight from the boat and Malcolm was allowed only one extra night's leave, for a honeymoon night before the journey to the hills and Eva's dramatic arrival at the manager's bungalow.

Before reading Eva's description of her arrival, one must again pause to remember the social position of 'the bride' in those days. For six months a bride reigned supreme, taking precedence, even to the extent of sitting at the right hand of the host at dinner parties. She might be married to a mere assistant but she was 'a bride'.

Can anything equal such an introduction to one's new life as a wild gallop along winding, narrow roads, bordered by tea bushes, out of which popped up one or two of the curious to see the new bride go by on a fourteen hand Bhutia pony, Peter, who had been waiting for hours in the cold and could now catch a whiff of his home stables. I was clad, not in the smart riding suit, with high leather boots which had taken a big toll of my trousseau money, but in an inadequate knee length dress as was the fashion of the time. The riding suit was, alas, following in one of my trunks carried by the team of coolies who had met us. Paul Revere could not have bettered that gallop, which ended finally outside the manager's bungalow, I to be presented in all my disarray and confusion as the new bride!

The following morning there was a two mile walk through a forest road down to a bungalow perched, like a pimple, on a small knoll which was to be our home for the next four years. A three roomed cottage, with a lean-to glazed verandah which we used as dining room, facing south. The centre room was the sitting room with two bedrooms leading from it, each with a so-called bathroom containing washstand, 'thunder-box' and tin bath inside a concrete curb with hole in the outer wall to carry away the used bath water.

In the kitchen, which led from the sitting room, was a reject iron stove of ancient lineage, fed by wood, a few shelves, a table of sorts and a sink on the floor. No water was laid on - a stand pipe was just outside the kitchen door, which was shared by all the servants and those living in the factory lines opposite. The factory itself was so close that it was possible to look straight into our home - the Factory Assistant certainly lived on the job!

The bungalow had only a corrugated iron roof with nothing to insulate it. In the winter it could be quite cold and we would have a wood fire, but we were allowed one maund of wood per day, which is 80 lbs for cooking, washing and hot water. This was almost inadequate since the bath-water was heated on a separate fire. In an estate surrounded by forest! However, we survived. In the rains the wood was always damp and everything was covered in smoke!

It was lonely, no other European living within miles. I would take the dogs for a walk in the evenings and be driven nearly mad in the monsoons with the noise of the cicadas, a sound which so maddened one planter that he took a gun and went out shooting into the air and the trees.

We were in a scattered community of ten or more tea estates of varying acreage, some run by the manager alone, others, larger, requiring two or more European assistants, who worked long, unscheduled hours with few privileges.

There were no telephones, other than inter-bungalow ones and they were few and far between. The dak-wallah (postman) was our public relations officer. His functions were of untold value. In the District there were only two post offices, one on each side of the valley. The dak-wallahs would congregate daily to await the arrival and sorting of the post from the main post office at the rail head. The dak-wallahs' first job was to exchange the communications between the scattered European neighbours, letters, small packages, rolls of newspaper and magazines which went the rounds from bungalow to bungalow and were so much appreciated even though they were months old. These, not going into the main postal system were unstamped. Letters to the other side of the valley had to be sent by hand and in one's early days it was obligatory to use the services of a young coolie.

The daily paper, the Statesman, already a day old would come from Calcutta. 'Home Mail' arrived on Monday so that Tuesday was a busy letter writing day to reply by return that afternoon and to catch the weekly boat sailing back to England.

Who could begin to estimate the amount of information gleaned by the Post Master, usually a Bengali, from each day's gathering of dak-wallahs? For one period of several weeks our letters did not arrive in England, the Post master had found what he considered a better use for the stamp money. He was eventually dismissed.

Nothing much to do, nothing else but noise of the cicadas to think about.

We had a cook - so called - and a bearer who looked after the sahib's clothes and the house generally and a water carrier, very necessary, for heating the kerosene tins full of water for our baths and as well as everything else which needed hot water in the bungalow; another very necessary adjunct was the sweeper who swept the bungalow and emptied the 'thunderboxes'!

The cook was not efficient but he knew the routine chota (small as opposed to burra - big) sahib's food, could kill a chicken if a visitor arrived unexpectedly by pouring vinegar down its throat so it would be tender, being killed at 5 p.m. and served at 8 p.m.

The first time that I was bold enough to attempt to make a cake I got him to stoke up the wood stove till the oven was a reasonable heat and I made a very good madeira mixture and put it into the oven and shut the door with instructions that it was not to be touched. Ten minutes later I went into the kitchen - there I saw both the cook and the bearer squatting in front of my cake, the oven door open. They were watching my cake - slowly being spoilt!

The servants could not speak English so I had to learn the language. Malcolm arranged for what was known as a Munshi (tutor) to teach me. He came in the evenings and made a vain effort to help me from his very small knowledge of the English language. After a few lessons I found I was doing far better without him than with him so we paid him off. Malcolm had learnt the same way. There were no text books.

The one great mistake I made over the language was probably a year after I had been in the bungalow when we had a visit from Padre Duncan, the Scots Mission Padre, a very loyal servant who rode miles round the country side visiting the Scots Mission Schools and all the Europeans and teachers that he knew. He asked me that evening how I was getting on with the language and I said tolerably well but, although Malcolm had a dictionary, I found a great fault in it - it did not give any indication how the words should be pronounced. When he had left the next morning, Malcolm said 'look in the fly leaf of the dictionary will you.' There, to my horror, I discovered that the compiler of this dictionary was none other than the Scots Padre, the Reverend Duncan. He was, though, a wonderful man and he worked fantastically hard.

The main provisions for the managers and assistants had to come from Darjeeling. Each household employed a 'roti wallah' or bread man for this purpose. At Tukvar the Roti Wallah would go daily to Darjeeling but from the Nagri district he could only go in twice a week. I had to rely entirely on my Roti Wallah since journeys to Darjeeling took too long and were almost unknown for the assistants except, perhaps for the great week-end when the planters had their Annual Meeting and dance.

It could be difficult, too, for supplies to be brought down during the monsoon. There were, however, supplementary Kayah shops on most estates which could be used. The Kayahs would allow some of the young men to run up rather heavy bills as another of the Kayah's functions was that of money lender. Some of the young men got into difficulties if not given adequate advice.

The Kayah was a plainsman, wore a dhoti and a pugri, and sold spices, bars of soap, cut by the yard, it was stored hanging in the shop and had a most unpleasant odour. He also sold sugar, rice, salt and matches. During the war, when there was no sugar we would buy ghur from him. This was the residue from the refined sugar. It was full of straw and dirt having first been trampled on by oxen before being clarified. It was boiled with water and strained and then set into a sort of thick molasses. It was very sweet, rather like brown sugar. We could make a sweet out of it although it did not set.

Except for salt and clothes the local people were fairly self sufficient. Each labourer's house had a small patch of ground where he grew vegetables and his corn, maize which was known as 'makai' - that was their staple diet. It was roasted on the cob and taken out for their mid-day snack while they were plucking or working on the estate. For their fires they made their own mixture of charcoal, dust and dung which they made into balls and they would also use wood which they gathered themselves. They kept the odd cow and we bought our milk locally. We sent up the bottles, usually two bottles a day. Nagri was an exception, because of the 'farm' and my milk came from the manager who rationed her strictly. It was part of the estate agreement that a number of cows be kept. That was quite exceptional.

117

As well as the house servants we also had a mali (gardener). He was an ancient minion who had a watering can and watered what little garden we had round the bungalow and he set off each morning up to the Manager's bungalow and bought back such vegetables as they thought we needed from their main vegetable garden. We had what was brought - perhaps three carrots - perhaps one cabbage very scanty - perhaps some had been lost on the way down!

There was also the travelling 'shop' provided by the Salvation Army. The Salvation Army provided work for the destitute who made embroidered table linen.

Their travelling salesmen would travel among the tea estates on foot accompanied by a man carrying samples of the goods they produced - goods unequalled for durability, table cloths, kitchen clothes, every kind of household cloth imaginable. The men made no arrangements for accommodation but one was glad to give them a meal or a bed for the night and to listen to their reports of work done.

One incident stands out in my memory to do with the Salvation Army - I was standing, on a railway station, with my baby, Ann, in her basket, surrounded by untold 'clubber' of bedding rolls, baby's equipment, picnic basket - imagine my reaction when a solicitous member of the Salvation Army approached and asked me if I was 'saved'! In fact I learnt to have an intense regard for the Salvation Army who did so much good work among the down and outs in Calcutta.

When I first arrived at Nagri Farm, Malcolm had a white Bhutia pony which he had bought on arrival, by name Tiddy. He had also bought Peter Pony, a brown Bhutia, young but of gentle disposition, ideal for initiating me into riding in the hills. This, of course, involved the employment of a syce (groom) for each pony, and grass cutters. Several evenings a week I would set off to the 'burra koti', the manager's bungalow, about two miles away, when Malcolm would be taking the daily report at the office. The pony would be sent back to his stable and quite often we were asked in for a game of bridge and would then walk home together, swinging a 'hat-butti', hand lantern, to guide our steps over the rough track, part of which passed through a stretch of jungle extending down to the plains.

One night as we left the verandah at the manager's bungalow we heard sounds of a leopard calling. The bearer said 'chitway' and the manager very nobly sent him to bring out his gun and a few cartridges. The cartridges Malcolm put in his pocket and reassured we set off to walk down through the forest. We saw and heard no more of the leopard fortunately, although the forest stretched right down to the plains and was a well known area for leopard. When we reached our own home safely we discovered, to our horror, that the cartridges did not fit the bore of the rifle. We returned both without comment!

For company before I came out Malcolm had two wire-haired terriers, Jimmy and Sue - good companions and always fun to take out for an evening walk. It was customary for the sweeper to give them a bath, at least once a week, usually on Sunday morning as Malcolm would then supervise the proceedings. One ghastly Sunday, when we had been out for lunch we returned home to find Jimmy's chain hanging loose, the sweeper must have left him chained to dry thoroughly, or perhaps even have forgotten him completely, and he had been taken by a leopard.

That there can be few if any animals more dreaded by natives than the man-eating leopard, is a view held by others besides Major F G Alexander who wrote in Harmsworth's Natural History. As he says 'Of all the beasts in India which I have studied and pursued, the leopard is the one for which I possessed the deepest animosity.' The same gentleman tells us that the leopard's motto is 'ubique' and one will find the animal in the most unexpected places.

Writing about her early days in India Eva continues:

Sometimes we were invited out for dinner. If it was during the rains, we would, as usual, carry our large umbrellas open and Malcolm would wear his khaki drill trousers over the black trousers of his dinner suit. I would ride up with my long skirt in a case and put that on when I arrived. It was quite understood that the women would change on arrival.

For the first two years or so I was able to visit neighbouring memsahibs on Peter Pony, also, once a month or so, I went with Malcolm to the Valley Club. This was a great expedition which needed great preparation. One set out in riding kit, tall boots and topi for an eight to ten mile trek followed by small boys with suitcases on their backs, containing suitable outfit for the church service, hat, shoes, also tennis kit and racquet. Since sandwiches were a taboo a further porter was required to carry all the impedimenta for a lunch and some burra-sahibs would even have a joint to carve. I remember my amazement at the first sight I had of the Club lunch table - tomato ketchup bottles stood in serried ranks the length of the table - everyone took his own ketchup! Everyone, too had his bearer to accompany the lunch to the Club and to serve his sahib and memsahib and the great burra sahib might even have two servants and sit down to a five course 'picnic'.

Before lunch on the Club day, each month, the district Anglican padre held a service in the little church and for that we were suitably dressed, having changed from our riding kit. The padre may have travelled quite some distance as his parish was extensive and widely scattered.

After lunch there was tennis on the two courts followed by tea. At dusk we changed into riding kit for the long journey home. An exhausting day but much appreciated.

One memorable night we arrived back later than usual to find the room and bedroom smothered in large, black, oily smuts from the oil lamps which the bearer had left for our return but which had burnt up in the draught. The sight of the turned-down beds was almost too much - everything be changed!

On another Club day Malcolm had gone alone and for tennis he was bedecked in a new pair of long white flannels which we had purchased at great cost. Being on his own, he had left rather late and still in his tennis kit. The pony who was fresh, had been waiting all day, and perhaps, who knows, the pony had a whiff of leopard as he set off. He went at a smart pace and stumbled in a puddle throwing Malcolm, resplendent in his white kit, into a bog. He arrived home covered in green slime from head to foot and as he sat in the tin bath tub I picked a jolly collection of nice fat leeches off his back till the bathroom floor was awash with blood!

Christmas was about a month after Eva's arrival at Nagri. This was the 'easy' time for the planters when the bushes were dormant, travel was easier and the weather, though chilly, was good. She describes the experience of her first Christmas:

The doctor, a charming Irishman and his wife lived another two miles further on from the manager's bungalow and they had laid on a Christmas lunch for six, Malcolm and myself, the manager and his wife and the doctor and his wife, neither of them had children.

In the middle - or almost before we had begun our lunch an agitated native came up from one of the lower divisions of the estate in great distress. His wife had been cutting firewood or looking at the corn and had been mauled by a bear. The sloth bears of the Himalayas used to haunt the corn as it was ripening and she had obviously disturbed this particular bear.

Christmas lunch was abandoned by the doctor who went off post haste down to the lower division. Sometime later he returned rather annoyed, the woman had been put on a machan (hard wooden bed) or stand outside her hut, she had been torn by the bear from her face down one breast almost to her stomach and had an open wound. They had not allowed the doctor to even put a dressing on the wound. He was only able to clean it. The woman had to remain outside the hut because the bear would have impregnated her with an evil spirit from its claws and until the wounds were healed the evil spirit could not be allowed into the hut.

It was quite a harrowing experience for one's first Christmas. The people in that area were animists, they had no Christian beliefs, though there was a mission school in the area. Animism was the strongest feeling.

After lunch we settled down to bridge. Soon afterwards the doctor was taken ill and unfortunately had to leave the District. He was a great loss and we all regretted his going. (As you will see he proved to be irreplaceable.)

GOVERNMENT HOUSE, DARJEELING, WAS SO SERIOUSLY DAMAGED THAT IT HAS HAD TO BE ENTIRELY DEMOLISHED.

17

Another Earthquake

Malcolm and Eva had three girls. The eldest and youngest were born down on the tea gardens. The arrival of each baby was accompanied by trauma of one kind or another which was not directly linked to that of birth itself. She recalled her experiences:

My first daughter was born in the bungalow. The district nurse, who Malcolm had known for sometime because she had lived in the plains and had been in Darjeeling quite often, arrived just the evening before Ann started up - Ann was early. The nurse had come up from the Plains and was developing denghi - a rather unpleasant fever so she was quite a sick woman before she had to leave me. What a friend that nurse was to be! The birth was difficult and the District Doctor, when he arrived, proved almost unable to cope with the situation.

It was a time of intense activity in the factory, Malcolm was working late and under strain. He damaged the first finger of his right hand in a machine, an accident which left his finger permanently disfigured. However, with the superb care I received, the babe and I soon began to thrive and with the on coming of the rains there was little incentive to journey far afield. I was certainly glad to be able to do without the ministrations of an inexperienced ayah.

After the nurse, Mrs. Milwright, left me Malcolm and I were with no one near to turn to for advice or help, though some of the other wives did visit. There was no clinic, of course there was the doctor and the Manager's wife but she was much older, had no children of her own and therefore little experience to call on.

The Doctor visited with his wife and to our great dismay when the wife was studying Ann she thought that she was going to be bow legged - because her legs were not straight - and she suggested that perhaps Ann should be put in splints. This distressed us terribly but fortunately before the Doctor could put his ideas - or rather his wife's - into action someone said 'Absolute poppycock, of course she's not, every baby's legs are bent till they begin to walk.'

It is awful to imagine what might have happened; this wretched woman was determined that Ann should have her legs broken and splinted.

One fateful night when I was giving Ann her ten o'clock feed by the bedroom window there was a loud scuffle, a whoof, a yap from a pi dog as the leopard carried him off, right under the bedroom window. Later on one of our own little terriers went the same way. Leopards think few things are tastier than dog. It was this awful noise, the scuffle and the pug marks on the bit of garden outside - nothing else.

Before Ann was a year old, Malcolm went down with para-typhoid - How? He spent a period in the 'San' in Darjeeling, where they saw fit to shave his head. He was still wearing his hair 'en brosse' when we went home in '30. I was always very sensible with hygiene. I boiled all the water and I, myself, saw that the milk boiled. I had no ayah - I looked after the baby myself - glad of something to do. I looked after the washing of the nappies but the sweeper would do them if necessary as we had only the well known thunder box which had to be taken away in a basket by the sweeper every so often to the distant cess-pit - a special destination - bore holes in the distant jungle. He took the deposits there - a primitive solution for the sanitation.

One of my nearest, and dearest, neighbours had given birth to a daughter, Annette, at about the same time. She proved an invaluable friend. When I again became pregnant and Janet was due, sixteen months later, she offered to look after Ann with Annette. For this advantage I had to engage an ayah. She was, I suppose, experienced, a large capable woman, but somewhat overpowering. For her meals Ann was seated on the floor, back to the wall, while ayah squatted before her and shovelled in the spoonfuls. Encouragement was given to Ann as she ate at speed, accompanied by "Belchy, belchy", when the inevitable effect was produced.

For this confinement the Doctor, who had had himself transferred to Darjeeling with its attractions of two clubs and an active bridge club, would not undertake my case unless I stayed in Darjeeling. As a result I had to travel there three weeks before the allotted date and stayed in a very indifferent boarding house. Fortunately I had again the care and services of the invaluable Mrs. Milwright.

Malcolm meantime was up to the eyes in the peak of the plucking season. Although he could visit Ann and report that all was well with her, he could not come up to Darjeeling as he was in charge of the estate - the manager being on leave. The doctor managed to arrive just a minute or two before Janet and so was able to claim his fee!

A dreary fortnight ensued at that depressing boarding house. I well remember one evening when Mrs. Milwright was off duty for a well-deserved break, my supper was brought to me, and she returned to find me sobbing into a disgusting mess of rice pudding which had been served up in those terrible aluminium pie-dishes of all sizes, which received such battering at the hands of the servants!

Before returning to Nagri Farm we had a Church christening at St. Andrew's Darjeeling at which my brother Bert acted as godfather. At that time he was an assistant at Soom.

Back on the estate we lived with our two little daughters in the Manager's bungalow, since he was on leave and Malcolm was Acting Manager; a pleasant local girl was installed as Ayah and responsive to my training; the lovely cold weather months lay ahead of us; oranges, pomelos, pawpaws, pineapples were delivered fresh from the orchard; I had a chicken run to supervise, White Leghorns and Rhode Island Reds gave us good eggs; and we had the space of the burra koti (big house). On Sundays, when we wished, there could be tennis parties.

One incident survives in my memory of this time - Janet used to sleep in her pram in the porch and once, to my horror, I found on one of my checking up visits that her nappy was full of blood! However, it proved to be a leech which had found its way into the pram and had enjoyed a good meal before moving on. Leeches were always a hazard.

Eventually time came round for our 'home leave' and we began the long trek to Calcutta, Janet was about nine months at the time. To make the journey up to the railhead Ann was carried on a specially made chair with a canopy to keep out the sun or the rain and a little place to protect her feet, she sat facing the way she was leaving. The baby was in a basket, strongly made, also on a coolie's back. We stopped at a godown or storeroom on the way to feed the children. When we reached Sukia Pokri we took a car along the cart road, the main road from Nepal to Darjeeling. This was a good, well made and well maintained road, not tarmacked, of course. There were always piles of stones at the side of the road for repairs and one saw the stone breakers sitting at work breaking up the stones. When we reached Ghum we took the narrow gauge railway, like a Welsh train, that sort of size and carriages. The railway twisted its way out of the mountains to Siliguri. The journey took about six hours. At Siliguri, in the Plains we transferred to the broad gauge and the express to Calcutta. We travelled through the night to arrive in Calcutta in the morning. For that journey we booked a four berth sleeper, we took our own bedding rolls, which the train attendant set out for us, some people would take their own servants with them. There was a bathroom attached to each carriage which was self contained, there was no corridor.

We arrived in Calcutta in the early morning after seeing the dawn break across the plains. It was flat after the mountains and as day broke we saw the Indians from the little villages going off into the bush to perform their early morning duties.

From the railway we went to the docks and embarkation. We sailed from Calcutta since it cost too much to sail from Bombay. The great thing for the assistant was that it took six weeks to get home from Calcutta but during that six weeks he was on full pay and everything was supplied. We had a six months leave with ten or twelve weeks taken up with travel - on full pay - it was a good way of saving and it was quite a consideration, whether one was sea sick or not, on one's first leave and with two small children.

After home leave we settled down to family life at the Beich Koti. In 1931 Malcolm sold his white pony, Tiddy, and we took over a larger pony, Black Bird, an Australian polo pony which my brother had had.

For their first form of transport the children had donkeys, at first with a ring saddle for safety but that was soon discarded as unnecessary. On a donkey they could travel quite a distance. At one time we had three in the stables, but if one happened to be left behind, possibly not required, we would be followed on our way by an incessant "Hee-haw" responded to by the more fortunate choice who was taking the children for a ride.

The best beloved was Saucy Sue a sturdy donkey, willing to submit to any indignity. She was loaned throughout the district as children went on leave or were sent to school. Because she had no "figure", the new owner would be convinced that she was pregnant, so Saucy Sue always had a pleasantly relaxed spell until the new owner became convinced that work would do her no harm!

The next step was a child's piebald pony called 'Whitelegs' - an ideal child's pony. This pony had once belonged to the Godden family when they spent the hot weather on a tea estate in Darjeeling. 'Whitelegs' is mentioned in one of Rumer Godden's books, "The River" I think.

My day began at 5.30 or 6 a.m. according to the day's programme, never later than 6, with tea bought to my bed by the bearer. Before breakfast I would see the milk strained through muslin and boiled, this

I watched sedulously each morning and then it was put into low bowls and stored in a cool cupboard covered with muslin. (There was no ice) Then the water boiling. The cook had a filter for his vegetable water, a small one, but I used a larger one in the outer pantry for the drinking water. It was into this that I next supervised the pouring of the meticulously boiled water. The water was then filtered and the filter water was again boiled in a special kettle, a very large enamel one which was kept specially for drinking water. This was a firm programme which I watched everyday.

The kitchen area consisted of an outer pantry where the shelves for the crockery were and then another pantry which led into the dining room or living quarters and that was where I kept my drinking water filter and where a lot of the preparation for anything for the table was made, and where I would mix my cakes. Some bungalows had their kitchens detached from the main building. This was not always desirable since it became a club house, not only for the servants, but for all their friends. It did, however mean that the smells from the kitchen did not permeate into the dining room.

I would also see the cook in the morning. Tell him if we were having guests or going out and give him the meal orders and his supplies which were doled out fairly generously.

When Malcolm returned from the factory, where he had been for several hours, we would have breakfast. The rest of my day was spent looking after the children, going out - taking them for walks, visiting the vegetable garden and interviewing the gardener, doing the flowers, looking at the plants - whatever happened to turn up.

Looking after the children included teaching them to read - when they were older. I joined a PNEU system for parents which was based somewhere in Cumberland I think. We got a monthly issue of lessons and opportunity to enter them for tests and exams. I did this for two or three years. It was quite comprehensive. It is probably still in operation.

Then my third daughter Jennifer was due. She put in her appearance on January 2nd, 1934. While I was otherwise engaged Ann and Janet were taken care of by a friend. They returned home one fateful Monday morning, The day was January 13 just ten days after Jennifer's birth.

Janet was under the weather with a fairly high temperature and went to bed. Ann went with the ayah to a lean-to, glass fronted room we used as a playroom, she was glad to be back with her old familiar toys. Due to the excitement of Ann and Janet's return home I was rather late starting Jennifer's two o'clock feed and was sitting in front of a rather dreary fire with only a coat over my shoulders when the earthquake came. Absolutely alarmed I fled, just as I was, out of the building, called the ayah to bring Anna out and she also went back into the bungalow to fetch Janet whom she carried out as a brick fell on her shoulder. In fact the first fall of sundried brick had fallen into the pram on the verandah, in which, had I been punctual in feeding, Jennifer would have been lying!

I stood out in the garden, my coat slung over my bare shoulders, clutching the tiny babe for what seemed an interminable length of time while the earth rocked and one wondered what was best to do.

The walls of the bungalow crashed down around and beside us. Malcolm was on the garden, the estate, he had not realised what was happening except that the pony seemed a little unsteady, he was actually out of the saddle at the time looking at the work that was being done. Shortly afterwards he returned and saw the damage. The walls had all collapsed and the floors were deep in all the rubble, there seemed to be nothing left.

The manager was living in the sturdily built mission bungalow half a mile up the hill. He was in Calcutta at the time of the earthquake. But his bungalow was standing and by evening we had transferred what we needed and as much as we could into this bungalow - that was what we could salvage, which was not a lot other than Epsom Salts for the ponies and we camped there.

Another description of the earthquake is that of Frank Evans, who, like Malcolm was out on the 'garden' at the time of the quake. He wrote to his fiancee, Grace, in England of the ripple effect, which was not unlike a stone being thrown into a pond. He was at the top of the estate and he saw the ripples going down and everything collapsing while the ground waved beneath him. Then the factory came down and when he returned to his bungalow he found only one wall standing.

At Tukvar the 'burra koti' had, it will be remembered, originally been the church where the Moravians had hoped to establish their self-supporting mission. After they moved out, the bungalow for the new Tukvar tea garden was built on and round the church, which was the dining room when I was there. In the days when my parents went there after the earthquake it was much as it had been for the first tea planters who lived there when the cookhouse was attached to the dining room. In those days all the rooms were dark, always. The windows were not large enough and the walls were very thick and, at the front of the bungalow, sheltered under the roof which covered the veranda.

After their home had collapsed and they had retreated to the 'burra kothi', Eva and Malcolm were soon joined by another who had walked down from their shattered home at the top end of the estate, Puttabong, close to North Point. Mary, being seven months pregnant had walked slowly down 2,000 feet with her mali (gardener) carrying a deck chair in which she took frequent rests. With her came her small son.

A few months later Eva and Malcolm were moved back to the Nagri valley but to a different estate, Chamong, where Malcolm was to spend the next six months as acting manager. The bungalow at Chamong had also been destroyed in the earthquake and the family spent the worst of the monsoon living in a wooden shack.

The homes which suffered most in the earthquake were those made from sundried bricks and which did not have proper foundations. The bungalow built by the German missionaries ninety years earlier had been soundly built. Most of the native huts survived because their simple construction enabled them to sway with the earth. Although it was a terrible experience for those who had watched their homes collapse, the overall damage was not as devastating as the floods. But for Eva, with her tiny baby and two other young children, the next few months must have been a nightmare. She herself has said little about this period, just mentioning that the family were moved to the ruined bungalow on Chamong Tea Estate, in the Nagri valley. This estate was on the borders of Nepal and, therefore, could only have neighbouring estates on one side and Seyok across the valley on the fourth side. It was a long walk and ride to Seyok.

The young family lived in a hut and because dry weather always precedes the monsoon, the wood from which the hut was built, dried out and shrank. When there was a hail storm, hail not only splintered onto the tin roof but came between the cracks of the walls to such an extent that the babe had to sleep indoors, in her pram with the hood up. The rain of the monsoon caused the planks to swell again and one problem was solved. Nothing, especially the wooden walls of a hut could keep the all pervading damp from everywhere and everything. Mould and damp was as much a part of the monsoons as the storms and rain. Even those hardy Loreto nuns were concerned with the level of the damp and the mildew on their books.

The monsoon was always a busy time for the planters, for it was now that the tea was growing well and manufacture was in full swing. As Eva says:

Note the plucking was at its height in the monsoon. The factory had a new Petter engine; Malcolm was an expert on Petter engines and every morning when it was time to start up the factory (which was usually between 3 and 4 am) a tap on the bedroom window and a voice

"Hazoor, hazoor" woke Malcolm up to come and start the engines for the driers as the leaf was ready to go down from the twithering racks. At a busy season when a lot of leaf was available he would often not finish till 8 or 9 at night.

An outing during the monsoon was always a risk because of the rains and if I went visiting I rode with an umbrella up. No mac could ever keep the rain out - at least riding with an umbrella meant that one arrived with dry shoulders.

Leeches during the rains were a menace. Once I was going out to a rather meticulously careful housewife for lunch and arrived on the doorstep with a fellow guest who just stripped the leeches from his stockings and shoes and stamped on them, leaving a blood stained verandah. I then found that my hand was bleeding, a leech had found its way up the horses flank, got into a small hole in the stitching of my leather glove, had his feed and dropped off leaving me to bleed inside the glove.

Malcolm was always badly bitten and as his old leech bites would irritate so he would scratch and soon his legs wore permanent scars from the sores which often went septic. Before my arrival and for some time after the Dr. Babu (every estate had a qualified medical assistant to tend to the welfare of the labour force) used to come in to "dress" the sores, a treatment which consisted of applying salt from a dirty screw of paper from his pocket! Hygiene was hardly an operative word!

When there was no motor transport there was a doctor resident in the district but later there was one doctor in Darjeeling and each garden had a 'doctor babu' - who was really only a 'compounder' and just knew the rudiments of the various diseases and dealt with the complaints of the labour - he had a training of sorts - Scots Mission again.

It was always a joke with us, as we walked through thick grass and undergrowth in the rains, that the one who walked ahead disturbed the leeches and the one who followed became the victim.

I do not think that Eva ever managed to solve the problem of Malcolm scratching his annual monsoon leech bites. They are as much a part of my childhood memories as eating mangoes. And I can well remember the Dr. Babu's daily visits. On one occasion, during the Second World War, the Dr. Babu was asked to attend to one of the family's numerous pets. The black labrador dog,

130

Tinker, had a hurt foot which had gone septic. The doctor and the patient were taken to a ramshackle veranda at the rear of the bungalow, with them went an audience made up of the resident children, which included my two sisters and myself, a friend Sally, who was a refugee from Burma, two French girls, whose parents were working for the Free French in what was then Indo-China, the servants, and to be sure there was no trouble, went Polly the parrot.

Polly may have been an ordinary, common green parrot but she liked to think that it was she who ruled the roost at Chamong. She was inordinately fond of Tinker, and therefore was most concerned that he should come to no harm. In fact to put it more strongly, it was only over her dead body that he would be hurt.

The foot was bad and it hurt the dog. The Dr. Babu was gentle in the extreme. He was careful but from time to time the dog would howl. At every howl the parrot waddled two or three steps forward, depending on the length or strength of the howl of pain. Finally she was within striking distance of his bare heel.

Parrots have a vicious beak, and this one was no exception. As everyone knew she had recently tested its sharpness on a visiting boy whom she thought was intending to take liberties with her person. None of us would have dared to touch her, she ruled supreme and was loved in our home. She had bitten her way out of every cage in which my mother had wished to have her contained, and now she faced the Dr. Babu.

Fortunately for the welfare of the Doctor's heel Polly understood what was happening, and however unpleasant, the treatment was for Tinker's good. However, there were, Polly considered, limits beyond which this man should not go. Fortunately for the Doctor, concentrating as he was on the dog and blissfully unaware of the approaching beak, that limit was not quite reached. The foot had been cleaned, a new dressing applied and all was over but so close was Polly that one, perhaps two more howls of pain and her beak would have been sunk into the Dr. Babu's bare heel - it had been a very close thing.

To return to the monsoon. As Eva says leeches were not the only problem during the rains.

Another problem during the rains were the leaking roofs. Because of the leaks, all the finger bowls and basins and every receptacle one could find was utilised. All rooms were littered with containers to catch the drips. It would probably rain for two days minimum then a short break and then it began again. There was the noise of the heavy rain on the corrugated iron roof not to mention the thunder and of course the lightning. Then, too, there was the mist and the drizzle which permeated everything. Everything in the house was damp and mould grew everywhere.

In the hills the monsoon dominated one's life. It affected everything. As a young, intolerant woman, I became obsessed with the damp and was miserable during the rains in Kalimpong, where I was working and where I suffered from mosquitoes (not the malarial variety). In two of my letters I wrote (15 June 1955):

Actually it is not raining at the moment. When the rain does stop and the sun comes out it is lovely, the sky is the most vivid blue. The other night we had a beautiful starry night and I could see right across to the lights at Darjeeling which was lovely. The sun too, when it comes out is very hot and everything begins to dry off and steams. My room has a leak in it which trickles down the wall to my cupboard which I take rather a dim view of as I am trying to keep my things dry. The only advantage is that my room is above the kitchen and so should be fairly dry. As soon as the mist comes down, which drifts into everything, it isn't really mist but cloud, I rush upstairs and shut my windows to keep it out and let the kitchen stove keep everything dry, then as soon as the mist clears I rush upstairs to open the windows to let the dry air in. Quite an exhausting business I find! It really is horrible how everything that one touches feels wet and sticky and horrible. Still it really is not as bad as that for when it is fine it is lovely.

(19th July 1955):

There was trouble at Tukvar last weekend when everyone was complaining about the rain and I said that I had managed to have two games of tennis in Kalimpong. When the bombardment had stopped I realised that the poor things hadn't seen any sun for the whole week. It was only then that I realised how lucky I was in fact to be working in Kalimpong where the rainfall is only about 90" while Darjeeling's is getting on for double that. However, this thought hasn't really cheered me up in the last day or so. It has been pouring down and except for a small break yesterday, but even so, we had to run for shelter under heavy rain. If I didn't have to move about I could shut myself up in my mouldy room, shut out the weather and forget it.

Well I am afraid that it is now Friday and I really haven't got very far with this letter. It still continues to rain and rain and rain. Even my typewriter now is mouldy which I can assure you is not through lack of use, as if I am not using it, Daisy is! Everything is wet and the whole house smells of mould and whiskers are growing on everything. Even cotton frocks which I put on feel wet and last week-end I put my jeans on to go home in and they were covered in nice smelly mould, and yet my room, being over the kitchen is drier than most. I feel that one morning I will wake up to find mould growing on my face. I can't think why I thought that it might be rather fun to experience a monsoon.

18

Of Leopards and Another War

It is incredible to us today, but some of the agency houses in Calcutta did not allow their assistant managers to marry until they had worked in tea for a minimum of five years, or in some instances until they became managers. Frank worked for one such agency and his fiancée, Grace, was still in England when he met Malcolm, or, to put it more precisely, when Malcolm accosted him on the state of the road he was supposed to be maintaining. It was because of the poor condition of the road that not only had Malcolm's pony stumbled, but he, resplendent in new white tennis flannels, was thrown into a puddle of green slime. Both men were keen tennis players, their differences were easily resolved and the resulting friendship was cemented by the fact that Frank's fiancée, Grace, came from the same town in England as Eva, Newark.

At the outbreak of war Grace was able to come to Darjeeling, ostensibly to stay with Eva, but in reality to marry Frank. So secret was their wedding, for fear that Frank lose his job, that the only one to know was Eva.

By the end of the 1930s when Grace arrived out in the district the standard of life for the Europeans had improved. All the managers of the tea estates and many of the assistants had cars. This made it easier to go visiting and for trips to Darjeeling, especially during the cold weather when the roads were less slippery or liable to landslides. For those with particularly bad or steep roads 'the baby Austin' had a particularly good bottom gear and with a specially modified back axle coped well with the gradients.

An increasing number of gardens were installing electricity and also improving their plumbing, thunder boxes were less common and some gardens began to boast of hot and cold running water.

A favourite 'plumbing' story of mine concerns a manager who boasted running hot and cold water in his bathrooms. It was quite true but the system only worked when the paniwalla was outside, with his cans, peeping through a hole in the wall and ready to pour the hot or cold water through the pipe as the guest turned on the tap!

Victorian manners and life style remained little altered, many always dressed for dinner even when alone and always when there were visitors, the men wearing evening dress and the women full length dresses. Even in 1954 I would have a bath and change into a full length housecoat for dinner.

Grace recorded some memories for me of her first few years in the Darjeeling area:

April 1938 I went out and was invited to Chamong where Eva and Malcolm were. We played tennis on the Saturday and played bridge at night and thoroughly enjoyed ourselves. I met Malcolm for the first time. Once a month we went to church, in the little church in the valley. The smallest church I have seen. This was followed by lunch. Saturday off into Darjeeling where Eva and I shopped. She showed me the bazaar and where to buy the different vegetables and a really very interesting trip. The children sat on their ponies while we shopped.

Then came the rains. This is a time, when the planters really are busy. The 'first flush' is not very good but in the Darjeeling District the second flush makes the most expensive and best teas. Many of ours at that particular time were sent to Russia.

During the rains visits were made to various gardens but it depended an awful lot on the weather. Often the roads, towards the end were washed away. Again, October, the start of the social life and the Governor came to Darjeeling, and we 'called' at Government House by writing our names in the book. I was taken to my first ball by Eva and Malcolm.

Another week I was taken to the Knight Errant Ball. This is a ball given by the bachelors in the district, really a way of saying, thank you to the managers and their wives who had entertained them during the rest of the year. During the ball they have their banners out and are dressed for the occasion in old fashioned dress knee breeches and tops.

I was married in '38 and in the spring of '39 had my wedding reception! Now I had to look to find my wedding dress - the dress I had been secretly married in six months before. Eva finally found it, down a rat hole - all torn to pieces! The reception was great - beautifully done, we had it at the Gymkhana Club, a dinner followed by my cake, decorated, of course, with two leaves and a bud.

When Grace arrived I was only four years old but I have some clear memories of the time. While I do not remember the hunt for the wedding dress, I do remember our first visit to stay with her and Frank when they were at a tea estate just across the valley from Chamong in the Nagri district. In fact I always really remember Frank in association with leopards. Being a shikari he was in demand when there was a dangerous animal around but as Grace has pointed out, one did not shoot leopards for their skins but because they had become maneaters and were threatening the lives of the labour force. As she says:

Frank did not shoot any tigers but he shot leopards. In the Doars, (the plains just below Darjeeling where there is a large tea growing area and where we were often stationed) it was the assistant or manager's job to shoot a leopard if it had been hurt for if it could not then shikar its own food it would go for human beings and we lost pluckers. This usually happened when it had a bad foot.

134

To prepare to shoot a leopard a platform would be built up a tree - and some live bait would be put underneath. Frank would then sit up in the tree and wait. At night the leopard would come and could be shot while it was eating the bait. The alternative to this method was to track it down, but this was always very dangerous. No damaged leopard was ever allowed on the garden - it always had to be shot even if it was chased for a week.

We were once at a garden where the manager had been taken very ill and we were asked to go and look after it. While we were there Frank went to shoot a leopard. It was three o'clock in the morning when I woke up to find that he wasn't back. I thought he was trapped up the tree so I borrowed the manager's very large car - ours was not big enough. Went down to discover that that was what had happened. The leopard had seen him up the tree, did not go for the goat and stayed there at the foot of the tree looking at him and Frank, unable to point the gun down sufficiently to shoot him, was stuck. Hearing the car come along it went off and Frank came down and left the leopard for that night.

The leopard has a distinctive dry cough of a call. This call was a frequent herald of evening when we were living at Singla. The tea, and the bungalow at Singla were close to the forests along the Rangit river.

These forests stretched into Sikkim as well as down river to the Terai and the plains. Of course, there were leopards in the Nagri Valley as well because there the forests went up into the Nepal hills as well as down to the Terai. Usually one just heard the leopard in the distance but one night I woke to hear one close by, so close I could almost hear him breathe. He was outside my bedroom window as he prowled round and round trying to find a means of getting at Tinker, the black labrador - there is nothing a leopard likes better than a tasty morsel of dog. It was no dream, in the morning the pugmarks were there for all to see.

The leopard's cough was not the only sound in those Darjeeling nights. Against the background of the frogs and cicadas were the bloodcurdling yowls of the rabies ridden jackal packs, while in the morning and early evening one was often pleased to hear the call of the barking deer, the small muntjac which lived in the forests. And from dawn till dusk there was the clarion call of the cockerel. Quieter but persistent were the buzzing of the flies and, in some places, the buzzing of the mosquitoes but, not surprisingly, it is the cry of the leopard which lingers in my memory most.

When driving at night one occasionally saw the beautiful, spotted beast whose cunning and cruelty is respected by all who have to deal with him. Safe, inside the car, it was always exciting. As Grace continues:

On another occasion we were going through a forest to have a meal with a garden about ten miles away and a leopard leapt out of the tea straight across in front of the car and went back into the tea. He was a very handsome creature. One only shot the leopards which were causing trouble not the ones which were just living their own little lives. Sometimes they were shot also because they became too many. Leopards are often shot because they raid the lines and the lines are the places where the coolies, the labourers live.

The very first night that Eva and Malcolm came to dinner Frank was in evening dress, in those days we did have evening dress for dinner parties, when he was called out to chase a leopard who had attacked someone in the garden. Just five minutes before we should have been sitting down to dinner, Frank arrived. The leopard was dead and, having taken his coat off, he was standing by it in immaculate evening dress.

I remember this particular occasion well. I was four years old, my two elder sisters, Ann and Janet were in England, at school, by this time, and I was on my own and had been put to bed. But there was such an atmosphere, for the servants were beside themselves with excitement, that however much Grace and my parents played the issue down, I was alarmed. The following morning I was taken out to see the leopard, dead. I do not think that I have ever been so frightened, I was quite sure that he 'would come alive and eat me'!

My next 'adventure' with a leopard was during the war when I had reached nine years and was big enough to be brave, or more precisely too proud to show my fear. My mother and I had been visiting friends several valleys away and were on our way home. The journey had begun with a walk down to a valley before we could ride up over the hill and walk down again to the Chamong bungalow. This trip took us all day and was of some interest because I was going through new country. For much of the way we rode through farmlands, belonging to the hill people. Most of the land was terraced, houses were scattered and everywhere the hillside was decorated by the bright red poinsettia growing like small trees. It is important to remember that the British did not make the whole area over to the tea planters but kept very substantial tracts for forest and equally large tracts were farmed by the hillman.

Near the valley bottom, on the edge of some forest, someone had set a leopard trap. If there was no one near by to shoot a dangerous animal this was the normal custom and a live goat is always put in at one end as bait. Our host accompanied us on our walk down to the river. In Darjeeling we never rode down hill, but walked and rode the ponies up hill. Someone once told me that no self-respecting Nepalese man would ride his pony downhill. As was the custom the ponies had been sent on ahead for our ascent up the other hill.

Planters did not usually go round their estates armed, and, as was usual, our host did not carry a rifle but knowing of the leopard trap, he wished, or perhaps thought we would be interested in a small diversion to investigate the trap.

When we arrived there was surprise, and, I sensed, some dismay that the trap was empty and the goat, the bait for the leopard, was still bleating mournfully. The pugmarks said it all. The animal had been there. His fresh pugmarks were not only clearly visible but testified that he was a wise old cat. He had investigated the trap, actually been into it and then turned away. I was convinced that he was lying up in the bushes just behind and that he would pounce at any moment, for such is his reputation. I could not feel reassured until we were on our ponies and several miles up the opposite hill. My mother appeared as nonchalant as everyone else. We all behaved as if it was a perfectly normal occurrence.

Leopards were not the only killers in the hills. Where it was low and hot enough, snakes could be found, particularly the cobras and kraits. One five foot common cobra was found curled round a pineapple close by the path at Singla bungalow and killed. It was on the previous day that I had been playing by the purple bougainvillea and found, and innocently played with, the cobra's eggs. Even the newly hatched baby cobra has the venom to kill. This huge bush was covered in flowers which reached down to the ground, but after the cobra incident the bottom two feet were cut away. At the same time the path surrounding the bungalow and the other flower garden paths, were covered in loose chippings, to make it difficult for the snakes, I was told.

Occasionally, as had happened at Eva's first Christmas, there were problems with bears and Frank's gun was again in demand.

On another occasion a message came to say that there was a bear attacking people in Nepal, just over the border. One side of Okati was British India and the other side was Nepal and in those days no one could go into Nepal, it was a closed country. But he was invited in to shoot this bear.

Just as Frank saw the bear up the hill it turned itself into a ball and rolled down the hill and landed in the river. Frank shot it and it got up again. He shot a second time and luckily it dropped. He discovered that the first shot had gone in at the ear, over the top of the skull and come out the other side. The Nepalese were very, very excited as bear fat is a great cure for some of their ills. They came down from Nepal and watched the bear being skinned and took away the fat and the parts they wanted for charms. The skin is now in England.

What Grace does not say in the above episode is that Frank was only able to get the second shot in after a furious race down the rocky river in which he injured his knee.

Not long after Frank and Grace were able to announce their wedding, war was declared and the younger planters began to be called up. Grace continues her description of life in Darjeeling:

The war years in India were very very busy ones. A lot of the troops came up for leave and they had the military hospital in Darjeeling. All the planters' wives really tried to help out by dancing with the troops at Government house and running a canteen. Eva was teaching in the school and for a while three of us odd wives stayed with Malcolm at Chamong.

Some wives came to Darjeeling from Burma - we did not know the women from Burma but one was marvellous at lengthening and shortening sleeves and sewing and goodness knows what. There was one who was pregnant and she was bitten by a dog and had to have the injections as a precaution against rabies.

World War II first came to Darjeeling as a recruitment drive for the tea planters and their labour force. The assistants and young managers left to join the armed forces and the Nepalese to join the Brigade of Gurkhas.

Malcolm also received his call up papers. He dressed in his NBMR [the Northern Bengal Mounted Rifles] uniform and with water bottle slung across his back, dug his heels into the side of his pony and set off for the wars. Before he had left the compound the telephone rang. The pony was pulled to a halt and Malcolm was told to stay where he was. The tea estate was on the frontier, someone should stay behind in the remote chance of an invasion from Sikkim or Nepal!

When London was bombed, the Europeans began to worry for their loved ones and most particularly for the children left behind at 'home'. Almost all of the planters had fallen in step with the Raj custom and had left their children in Britain for their education. No matter what it cost, both emotionally and financially, the sacrifice was made and children and parents saw each other but rarely, and then, as often as not, in hotel bedrooms, rented accommodation, or with grandparents. For the most part, family life ceased to exist when the children reached eight or ten years of age.

The authorities managed to arrange for the children of parents who were abroad to be evacuated out of England by sea. The great P & O liners were commissioned. Following instructions most of the childrens' guardians just dumped them at Liverpool Street Station. They did not know what was to happen to them and who was to look after them. One day a convoy slipped quietly out of Liverpool, on each passenger liner were hundreds of unaccompanied children. The ships sailed round the Cape of Good Hope, the voyage lasted about six weeks and the youngsters ran riot, being contained only by the railings round the ship and by the oceans. As far as parents or guardians were concerned, they had ceased to exist, until a telegram was received from the African port of Freetown giving their estimated date and time of arrival in Bombay.

One day the great liners steamed into Bombay proudly flying the red ensign, but there was not a yellow flag in sight, although not a single ship was free of an infectious disease. Their decks swarmed with excited children, waving madly. It was a sight Eva could never forget. That night seven trains pulled out of Bombay. They were packed with children and bound for destinations all over India.

The existing schools in Darjeeling were expanded and two new schools were opened, the New School and Singamari, a school just for girls with Miss Webb as the Headmistress. She came from one of the pioneering tea planting families. Eva, a trained teacher taught, ran her home, and a boarding house for girls during the term time. Other local wives did the same.

Burma fell to the Japanese and all were taken by surprise. Generations of Indian Civil Servants (ICS) had allowed themselves to be obsessed with the danger of the North West Frontier, forgetting that an eastern line also existed. There were no substantial military bases, almost no installations. In fact the eastern frontier had presented an open door, an invitation to the Japanese. The Japanese army took Singapore in a swoop and pressed on, sweeping into Burma. India had to act quickly on the eastern frontier. Roads and aerodromes were urgently needed, first for the withdrawal of troops and refugees and then for the offence initiative.

The Delhi Conference was held on 24th February 1942. The Indian Tea Association was asked to attend and was asked for help. It agreed to supply the largest possible number of tea garden labour for road building, the necessary number of Indian clerical staff and Europeans to supervise them. It also agreed to transport the 'volunteers' to site and to feed and maintain them while there, and this included all necessary medical facilities.

Only three days after the Delhi Conference, an advance party of one planter (from Assam), with 100 carefully chosen labourers with their own rations and medical supplies, had arrived at Manipur Road Station, in spite of the fact that it was some ninety miles away and it was the time of the Fagua festival. This advance party set out to prepare the reception camp for the 'real labour force' by making 'bivouacs' from jungle leaves and branches. As Sir Percival Griffiths says in his 'History of the Indian Tea Industry', 'Planters with labour from their own gardens now began to arrive and some were ready to begin just five days after the conference. Thanks to the remarkable co-operation of the Army and the Tea Association and the complete confidence of the tea garden labour in the planters, the miracle demanded by General Wood was accomplished.'

On 5th March Rangoon fell. 20,000 refugees were transported with only one fatal accident. That was the beginning of the combined task. The next was to construct roads, camps and aerodromes.

The saga of the Manipur and Leda roads, the achievements, privations of those who worked there is not for these pages. Though one of those responsible for organising planters was EJ Nichols - EJ as everyone who worked with the firm of George Williamson called him. Some of the terrain they worked on has

139

similarities with the Darjeeling roads: 'The next stretch was described by Pilcher as a fisherman's paradise and a motorist's nightmare, a ledge cut out of the almost perpendicular cliff with a sheer drop into a narrow gorge.'

The Darjeeling planters did their share, looking after each other's gardens and then taking their force of 'volunteer' workers off. When it was Malcolm's turn, Eva sent her husband off to the road armed with a tin of her special rock cakes and some pickled eggs, little knowing that that was to be his food for several days. Living in tents for weeks on end with only lentils to eat, was part of the experience while back in Darjeeling the streets were becoming crowded. First with the influx of European children, then with some of the Burmese refugees, the British troops on leave or to convalesce, and finally the Americans came to town.

Food became a problem and tracts of forest were cleared to grow vegetables, not just for Darjeeling, but for the Forces, and rationing was introduced.

The school holidays always lasted the three months of the 'cold weather' - December to February - and it was for one such period that Eva, on holiday from teaching, was running a household of her three children, a girl from Burma and two Free French children, whose parents were in Chungking fighting with the Free French. The crisis with the Japanese in Burma was such that no one could think of, let alone worry about, leaving the women and children alone on isolated frontier estates. So when Malcolm had left for 'the road' his wife and children came home to Chamong, isolated on the Nepal border and with a neighbour several miles away. They had no transport they could use, just their own feet and some ponies which they used for their visits to the Nagri Valley Club and to other gardens further away.

The food ration system for Darjeeling was simple, and based on the assumption that every household shopped once a day. For Eva and other isolated families on the tea estates this had never been the case. Twice a week, the roti (bread) walla, his basket on his back, took the steep short cut up over the hill to Darjeeling to fetch Eva's supplies and two loaves of bread per week was, therefore, her lot for the six hungry children in her care. Ration or no ration, twice a week was all the one man could manage and the supplies he could bring back from Darjeeling were limited to what he could reasonably carry in his basket.

Fortunately, there were home-reared chickens and eggs, milk and goats from the Nepalis, as well as the local atta, which Gwaler had been so desperate for in the Sikkim campaign. This brown flour was not unreasonable and made quite good scones. There was also pumpkin - with lemon or orange to make jam, pumpkin soup, pumpkin curry, pumpkin everything. For sugar there was 'goor', made from crushed cane in village presses, producing a form of crystallised molasses which was not unpalatable.

The British troops flocked to Darjeeling for leave or to recuperate after illness or wounds. The first train load arrived in the middle of winter, the troops shivering in their tropical kit. The residents of Darjeeling had to rally round with jumpers, coats and blankets, anything to help keep them warm while the authorities were curtly reminded that Darjeeling was cooler than Calcutta or Burma!

Canteens were set up at Ghum, the coldest station of all, and also at Darjeeling, dances and entertainment were provided and those tea estates which were within easy walking distance of Darjeeling were involved in entertainment.

Before the war came to an end, Malcolm was moved from Chamong, where Eva and the children had passed the cold weather alone. He was appointed manager of the large estate of Tukvar, which at one time had employed four assistants. I loved Chamong and tears had to be shed, very privately, all over the garden before we left, knowing, perhaps that we could never return. On one of our last mornings there, we were seated at a never-to-be forgotten breakfast. The meal was in progress when we heard a shot. No-one spoke, no-one cried and no-one could look another in the eye. We all knew that our beloved Peter Pony was dead. Too old, too tired to make the long journey to Tukvar we could do no more for our faithful friend than to ensure that he would not suffer. He was shot, as was the custom, standing beside the grave I could never visit.

Although it was hard to leave Chamong, the move to Tukvar was, in essence, one of coming home. The family, which included the dog, parrot and rabbits amongst its menagerie, soon settled down happily on the estate which stretched almost to Darjeeling's North Point and within reach of the bright 'city' lights as well as down to the orchard of mangoes and oranges and the forest by the Rangit river, that delightful and beautiful picnic spot four thousand feet lower.

There was some luxury, too, in the bungalow whose first walls had been built by the Moravians just a hundred years earlier. Not only had it withstood the earthquake, but it had been modernised. The factory, and also the bungalow, now took its electricity from the main supply in Darjeeling. The hot water was now heated by electricity, no more did the paniwalla have to heat cans of water over a wood fire before carrying them to the four bathrooms. Now we could just turn on the tap.

The old cook house had been demolished to extend the veranda and allow more light into the dining room, once the church. A new cook house, which contained sinks for saucepans, vegetables, crockery and glasses was built as an adjunct to the hall and where it would not prevent light from reaching the reception rooms.

To improve the sittingroom, two large bay windows were added to look out onto the front garden. The managers always surrounded their homes with large, beautiful gardens, and ours at Tukvar was no exception. In their season there would be walls of sweet peas with as many as six flowers on each stem, rows of chrysanthemums, prize winning dahlias, the blooms were so big, shrubs of the red flowering poinsettia and hibiscus not to mention shade-giving trees festooned with wild orchids. Most days the roti walla had his basket filled with flowers to take to a Darjeeling hospital and large bowls of fresh flowers stood in every room.

At the back of the bungalow, the side of the bedrooms, was my favourite tree, an old walnut, covered in moss and with branches festooned with orchids. A swing had always hung from one of its spreading branches to be used by the resident child. I had been passing the morning with a book up in this tree when lunch was announced. It was a hot, headachy day when everyone is cross. Halfway through an ordinary lunch the table began to shake. With a reflex bound we were all outside but the earth tremor, which had, for an instant alarmed us, was but one of those sent from time to time to irritate but not to harm, and we returned to the half eaten meal.

To help warm the sittingroom during the cold winter evenings a new fireplace was built at the same time as the other alterations were made. It was built to the latest Calcutta fashion in a pseudo marble mixture. Unfortunately the experts who came up from Calcutta did not realise that this fireplace was not just for show but was for use and left salt or some such vital ingredient out of the mixture. The first fire to be lit cracked the fireplace from top to bottom. A great shame. It was never mended and somewhat spoilt the grand effect!

Nothing was done to the east end of the bungalow except to remove an old stove out of the corner of the office cum breakfast room. The large windows looked out onto a hedge of white Australian tree daisies and faced down towards the stables and up towards Darjeeling's North Point. The windows were large and needed no altering. They allowed the morning sun to fill the room as we ate breakfast, as my father gave the letters to the postman, and as Jimmy, the black Tukvar tom cat slept after his night out. A real cat, rat and bird catcher, Jimmy never made friends with Tinker the dog, but died of old age before Eva and Malcolm finally left in 1955. And in the corner as always, was the nest of the house martins. Every year they raised their young, and every year at least one window would be left open so they could fly in and out. When they had first settled I don't know, but they were as much a part of the house as the bricks and mortar.

At the west end of the bungalow a large semi-circular room was added. This was a modern, light airy room with large windows looking out onto the snowy range and one of the best views in the district. Here, watching the sun set over Kanchenjunga, Eva entertained battle weary troops to 'tea'. Not the traditional high tea of Britain but a compromise between something reasonably substantial and the delicate cucumber sandwiches, scones, buttered toast fingers and cakes which was the custom for managers' wives to produce. A meal to be served in a sittingroom with sugar lumps and awkward tongs, and with impossible napkins, smaller than serviettes, more like a lady's handkerchief and with lacey edges. Napkins which in former days had been bought from the travelling salesmen of the Salvation Army and worked by women in need. These tea napkins were as much a part of tea garden life as were the black ties and long dresses of the dinner tables.

But when the clouds were down a more sensible meal would be laid round the large diningroom table! An arrangement which must have been much more comfortable for the guests.

During the first few months at Tukvar, Eva had kept 'open house' but since she was also teaching full time in Darjeeling she soon found that it was best to be 'at home' every Monday when she had a half day and could walk down the 2,000 feet from Singamari School. A group of troops would come down early in the afternoon and be shown round the factory by Malcolm before being entertained to 'English tea'. They would usually order ponies for the 2,000 feet and five mile climb back in the evening. As they lingered over their tea, reluctant to leave an English home, or perhaps face the road and the ride back, Malcolm would begin to tell his animal stories - first the snakes and then the leopard ones till finally soldiers took the hint and left.

There were always strangers around at home now when we came back from school. The group of sailors who came were easy, they just wanted lettuce and as more and more was fetched from the vegetable garden I could not have cared less. Then there was the group who arrived, unexpectedly, just as we were experimenting with our new refrigerator, and I was about to taste ice cream for the first time. The ice cream was given to the visitors and I was told I could have more another time! Then there were those who came to stay for several weeks like the butcher's boy who was happy to help 'cull' my pet rabbits. Having started with two, 30 was a trifle excessive and I had not bothered even to name most of them, but our 'guest' should not have taken the biggest, Benjamin Bunny!

During all the war years we kept our car but with severe petrol rationing, the impossibility of replacing worn tyres, and other problems it was rarely used. There were, as always, the ponies. At Tukvar we housed young polo ponies belonging to a neighbour who was killed in action, an old mare, Judy, who replaced poor Peter Pony, and Merlin, a racehorse from the Calcutta race track who had a vicious temper, and had obviously been badly treated. Merlin was a delight to ride and in time, responded to our gentle treatment. We did not miss the car. In fact it was of less use to us children than it was to Malcolm because we could never be driven to Darjeeling in it. So severe was the gradient that the car could manage but one passenger, Eva, while the rest of the family always rode up the hill. Walking and riding had always been a way of life on the tea gardens.

For the town itself transport was, as it had been since the early days, nothing less than a problem during the war years. There was an indifferent road, and the DHR or toy mountain train as the main means of communication with the Plains. This system was stretched to the limit particularly during the monsoon. The old, original road, the one that Lloyd had plotted and Napier had finished building was still used by those prepared to walk but it could not take wheeled transport. That the town and District in general was able to cope at all during the war years was to its credit especially as there was no ropeway, as at Kalimpong, to help ease the load.

The first ropeway to be installed was at Kalimpong and was opened in 1930.

The ropeway connects with the Tista Valley branch of the Darjeeling Himalayan Railway at Rilli after crossing the Tista and Rilli rivers. It rises 2,500 feet to Kamesi where there is a 72 H.P. engine to drive the lower section, a distance of 4 1/2 miles. From Kamesi the ropeway goes in a straight line of 2 1/2 miles to Kalimpong, at 4,100 feet where there is another 72 H.P. engine. Baled wool, oranges, timber were carried down while up came food-grains, brick-tea, cloth and building materials.

In 1939 another ropeway was opened and ran from Darjeeling to Bijanbari, which is an important trade centre from eastern Nepal and western Sikkim and for some tea estates. Potatoes, vegetables, poultry, cardamoms and forest produce being carried up and cloth, yarn, sugar, salt, kerosene and metals down. This ropeway was powered by two 24 BHP diesel oil engines and ran over a distance of five miles.

The head of the ropeway was on the cart road to North Point and Lebong and we drove past it regularly on our way to Tukvar. Because the managing agents, Messrs. Goenka & Co sold petrol, Shell petrol as I remember from the golden shell suspended by the road, we were regular customers. Over the years other, 'private' ropeways were added powered by a variety of sources from water, electricity, hydro-electricity and just plain gravity. There were two at Tukvar, an old gravity feed one which was used to transport the newly plucked tea leaf from the top of the garden down to the factory and the new, powered one, which ran between the factory and North Point, where it was on the main cart road. This was a great improvement as it carried the heavy tea chests up which formerly had been transported by pack ponies and it brought the food for the labour down.

It was not long after the Tukvar Ropeway had been built in the early days of the war, when a woman, for some rather desperate reason, decided to 'hitch a lift' on it and sat on one of the open trays. She can have had little idea of what she was doing since the trays were not designed for passengers, there was nothing to prevent one falling off if one took a dizzy spell having looked down into the bottom of a ravine. The first part of her journey was fine, but it was a misty day and when the engine was shut down, the day's work being over, this woman was left, suspended in space. The only person to hear her cries was the almost deaf engineer who was working in the factory. It was his distorted hearing which was able to pick up the pitch of her screams from the noise of the factory machinery. First the engineer had to persuade everyone he was serious, but he was insistent that he could hear a human cry. The engines were started up and eventually the tray loomed in out of the mist with its very cold, frightened passenger. Malcolm once hitched a lift up on it. Being very busy he had either forgotten, or was late for, a school function at Singamari and decided that the ropeway would solve his problem. He was ashen and shaking when he arrived at school describing how the tray would tilt and he would look down into the depth of a forest clad ravine.

The ropeway and the factory at Tukvar were powered by electricity brought down from Darjeeling. With so much rain, rivers and water, it is not surprising that Darjeeling claims to have had the first hydro-electric undertaking in India, with the original plant being set to work on 10th November 1897. However it was not until the 1930s that electric power was introduced to most of the tea estates. Being not too distant from Darjeeling, Tukvar decided against its own generator, as became the custom on most gardens, but plugged direct into the town's supply. The result was a surprise. The first time the factory, with its new electrical machinery, was switched on, Darjeeling blacked out. There was a solution to the technical problems but every time Tukvar wished to start up the machinery in the factory a phone call to the power station in Darjeeling had to be made first!

And what a luxury this electricity was. Not only did it mean being able to iron a dress from time to time, it meant hot baths when it suited. Before that hot water for the bath had come from a boiler some distance from the bungalow and stoked only in the evenings. And before the pipes were laid to the modern enamelled baths, we used tin tubs, the paniwalla having to carry the cans of near boiling water in for us. Tin tubs, however, lingered on in many places and even as late as 1954 when I was living in the very modern and English looking Jubilee House at the Kalimpong Homes I bathed in a small oval tin tub. This was also still the practice at the Himalayan Hotel in Kalimpong.

But this hotel was unique and tin tubs were part of its tradition and atmosphere along with a charcoal fire set in the middle of the living room to prove how efficient this old, Tibetan form of heating is. This sigri gave off, as I recorded in my letters, no smoke but a great deal of heat and being central in the room was most comforting and warm. I did not recall whether there was a 'lights out' time at the hotel, there was at Jubilee House where the lights went out at ten. This was also true on one or two of the estates I also visited at this time. For unless one's garden was near enough to be supplied direct from Darjeeling, the electricity supply remained a bit primitive. When we were at Chamong during the war years we only had power for the evening. The radio was operated by battery which was usually re-charged in the evenings and we soon learnt that if we wished to use the new iron we would suffer a blackout from blown fuses unless we ensured that most of the lights and the battery charger, in particular, were switched off.

Apart from the cow dung fuel which one saw drying outside every Nepali home, we burnt wood on our open fires and mostly in the cooker, a large woodshed usually being placed beside the substantial chicken-house and runs. During the war years with so many extra people around, the consumption of the charcoal one sometimes saw being made in the forests, increased from 150,000 bags to 350,000 bags per annum. The cost too, doubled. No wonder the forests were depleted. But the war over consumption plummeted down as the Darjeeling streets emptied, as the troops left along with most of the European children who were gradually returned to their schools in Britain leaving the district to look ahead to Independence.

The Teesta valley mail

19

Postwar Years

The end of the Second World War brought considerable changes to Darjeeling. Ice was made in the fridge and some people even had air-conditioning. Calcutta residents could now cope with the heat and had less need to escape to the hills. Air travel made it possible to travel back to Britain quickly as Malcolm did in 1946. He flew in a sea plane, a most comfortable form of transport. The journey took several days, as opposed to weeks, with a final touchdown in Southampton Water.

The troops and most of the British children, including my sisters and myself left Darjeeling. The now almost deserted streets promised less prosperity to the tradesmen. There had to be readjustments. The tea industry feared labour troubles and shortages as the day for India's Independence approached.

The situation is well summed up in the Minutes of the Darjeeling Planters Association at their meeting on the 2nd March 1946 at 11 o'clock. It was the 73rd Annual General Meeting and the first since the end of the six long years of war. In the opening remarks of his address the Vice President, Mr. Malcolm Betten said:

> In this great struggle, of the second world war, we have, as an Industry, been privileged to play our part. A high percentage of Planters served with the armed forces and we are proud of the fine record they have earned. ...We take pride in the fine record of the Gurkha Battalions whose heroic exploits have won world wide admiration and in whose ranks hundreds of our garden boys served. In the spring of 1942 when the enemy had reached the frontier of India, the part played by the Tea Industry in the evacuation from Burma, the building of roads and other military projects, is one of which we as an Industry might justly be proud.
>
> During these war years we have had to face many problems, labour was short on practically all Estates, essential stores were difficult to obtain and above all there was the constant anxiety of obtaining sufficient food for our labour.
>
> I wish to-day that I could say that our worries were over, but we know only too well that greater problems loom ahead...

The 1945 crop in Darjeeling was generally speaking a poor one. In some Districts hail storms caused much havoc. In these hills we rely on early rain for our Spring crop. On some Estates as much as 30% of the crop is harvested by the end of May and drought during the early part of the year was mainly responsible for the low outturn.

...With the release of men from the forces, coupled with the fact that labour will no longer be required for military projects or vegetable farms some improvement in the position is to be hoped for.

There is one fact gentlemen we must not lose sight of, are the men now returning prepared to accept conditions as they were before the war?

...During the war years the difficulty of obtaining coal has resulted in the depletion of Forests in this District. We realize of course that this was unavoidable, but it will be a serious matter for this District if re-afforestation is not pushed forward vigorously.

...We have two main roads, Siliguri to Darjeeling and Siliguri to Kalimpong via the Teesta Valley and the Darjeeling Himalayan Railway runs on the same alignment as these roads.

Slips on the line and road are frequent and serious dislocation of the traffic results. Such a slip occurred on the Teesta Valley rail line and road and was a serious matter not only for the Tea Industry but for Kalimpong, Sikkim and Tibet and the many smallholders who needed transport for perishable goods. After the cutting of much red tape this road is now opened, can we be assured that all possible steps are taken to see that this vital line of communication is being safeguarded?

With the exception of the Teesta Valley the carriage of tea and stores by the Railway was satisfactory and our thanks are due to Mr. Martin [is this a relative or just co-incidence of the one of Hope Town and Bycamaree one must wonder?]

Our road and rail are our life line and a hold up in the flow of traffic may have such serious consequences that an alternative route is essential. With the road developments which must now be undertaken this is a necessary safeguard in our communications.

Most gardens are far distant from their railheads and are served by what can only be described as winding tortuous tracks. Yearly we have

148

Tukvar Tea Estate. Malcolm Betten at table; Nepalese Assistant Ram Krishna at front (c.1950)

to expend thousands of rupees on the most primitive means of transport, the backs of human beings, pack ponies and bullock carts. A state of affairs which we should no longer be prepared to accept. We realize that during the war years shortage of labour and material made it impossible to develop and even maintain our present roads, as we know to our cost, as practically all our cars are scrap metal through use on the Grand National Course which constitutes our highways.

In this age of Atomic Energy we do not wish to see the present tooth pick efforts, two men to a crow bar, hundreds of human beings rolling in poor metal [stones], while modern diesel engines rust by the roadside...

Eight years later the situation had not changed much. On Tukvar, lorries carried the tea up from the Singla section to Tukvar from whence it went by ropeway to North Point. These lorries could not negotiate the road above Tukvar and so just plied between Tukvar and Singla, a distance of six miles and a drop of around 2,000 feet. I experienced the 'quality' of these lorries only once. I had walked with a companion from Teesta Bazaar, which lies at the foot of Kalimpong, through the forest beside the Teesta to its junction with the Great Rangit where some ponies met us for the journey up 2,000 feet to Singla bungalow. From here we were to go in the estate lorry up to Tukvar. Of this trip I wrote:

> Then after tea the three of us, John, Allan and myself climbed into the oldest of our two lorries, me in the front, and John and Allan standing precariously behind. I had been joking at tea and saying that the lorry was more comfortable than the jeep and I wouldn't need a cushion, but oh I wish I had taken one. I hadn't been in this lorry before, the other one has a thin piece of cloth over the hard boards, which lessens the blow to one's 'beau hind'! Actually John and Allan were lucky to be standing in the back because they could not see how admirably well the foot and hand brake worked. The hand brake didn't even pretend to work, and the foot brake only did when the mood was on it.

> I will say these Nepalis are extremely good drivers. When we had to reverse round a corner we did so on the clutch, a nice feeling when there is no wall behind! The engine was soon boiling so we stopped to fill up with water and on we went for another quarter of an hour. This time we stopped on the steepest bit of the hill we could for more water which was poured in and all over the engine flooding something it dinna ought to flood and the darn thing wouldn't start again. Quite unperturbed the driver put the thing into reverse and we all careered backwards down the narrow and steep track. At this point I noticed that

the tea bushes growing down the hillside had recently been pruned and looked like so many spears upstanding and waiting to receive us.

Backing did not start the lorry. It was dark now and a candle would have done better than the headlights, but someone lent us a torch and the driver fiddled about for a bit, (everyone passing was most friendly and helpful). Eventually the driver got back in, let the brake off again and we careered down the hill backwards even faster than before.

Well it started! The driver played around with the accelerator, perhaps to reassure himself that the engine really was alright, to me it sounded so awful that I did not think it would be able to move the lorry down hill, but we were soon off and I realized that it always made that noise.

That experience was during the dry weather, during the monsoon, motor travel was always more exciting and one of my first experiences of the hill roads was soon after I had arrived back. The monsoon had just not quite finished and some of the roads were liable to be slippery or suffer from fallen trees or rocks.

On Wednesday night after I arrived we went to a party given about two hours drive away. Distance here is nothing, it is the time it takes to get there which is important. Tukdah, which is in a different valley from that of Tukvar, isn't really very far away it is just that one is climbing all the time on a very very twisty road. We climbed from 4,000 ft up to nearly 8,000 and then down again to 4,000 ft just to get there. Half way down on the road there was a truck drawn up and two people from the club were serving out hot rum punches in cups made out of bamboos. It really was wonderful and put us all in the spirit of things! The Tukdah Club was originally the officers mess of a cantonments there. The party was held at the Tukdah Club where we danced to a cranky old gramophone playing cranking old records, but it was tremendous fun. The walls of the hall were covered with heads of the odd leopard, tiger, boar and various other animals. These were dressed with collar and ties, the ties made of paper but painted both sides representing that of the Indian Tea Association. It was surprising how much like some of the older planters these animals looked.

We got home at three the next morning after great fun and games.

The car in front of us had broken its fan belt, and did the whole trip without one, our back lights weren't working and we were nearly run into when we were forced to stop after having run over the branch of a tree which was across the road and got caught up in our under carriage. We ended up going in front of the car with the broken fan belt so that they could use our headlights. There is never a dull moment here.

A week or so later I was invited to the Nagri Valley to play tennis, and the trip being further than the one to Tukdah I was given a bed for the night at Nagri Farm Burra Koti, Eva's first destination more than thirty years earlier.

Last Wednesday got up at crack of dawn and went up to Darjeeling. I was going a mere 25 to 30 miles, if that, to the Nagri Club for an American Tennis Tournament.

First it was up to Darjeeling where I met two planters and we proceeded by taxi to Ghum railway station. There we waited quarter of an hour to be picked up by an A40. I will here pause to say that the two planters I was with each had cars, one hadn't a battery and the other was being overhauled. It was supposed to be ready, but the day before it had gone out on trial on the end of a tow rope!

The A40 we were now in, or had been shut into, had no shock absorbers, the doors only opened and shut from the outside, the windows had lost the handle to turn them up so they remained open. We then set off on the next lap of our journey! We went along a very good road. It had no tar macadam surface and was very very dusty and bendy but as roads go out here it was good. After a while we met my host and hostess coming in to Darjeeling so we stopped to say 'how do ye do' and 'see you at midnight' then off we went again. We soon came to the bazaar of Sukia Pokri and bumped our way through it over various dogs, children, shops and boulders! Here we turned off into the forest and bumped our way over more boulders and bends down the hill. I forgot to mention that the bottom gear of this car had nearly had it.

After an age of this road we emerged at a junction and bazaar. Here a jeep was awaiting us and here six of us, six trunks and six tennis racquets piled aboard the small jeep. The party of four was now augmented by a driver and what the other lad was doing I don't know. We now proceeded down a road which in my childhood had not been a motor road merely a pony track, I don't think they have done much to it since but a jeep can go where the old baby Austin couldn't!

We were careering down the steepest part of the road about to charge a blind corner when a jeep popped round. We stopped with an inch to spare and then we began to manoeuvre. Of course it was quite impossible for either jeep to back any distance so we wriggled past each other, but not before the upward going jeep had run backwards

152

down the hill to start the engine! These jeeps seem incapable of starting normally. The favourite way to start is by running backwards down a steep hill on a road just about wide enough for a bicycle and with a steep drop one side. I love it when it begins to bounce too!! After about half an hour of this road we had to abandon the jeep and take to our feet for the last quarter of a mile.

It surprises me now that they thought this road not fit for a jeep after what we had been down!

The tennis was very poor, but tremendous fun as also was the party afterwards. At 11.30 in pitch darkness with pruned, spiky tea bushes on either side I walked up a different path for half an hour before meeting the landrover which was to take me to Nagri Farm. Here I met my host and hostess, now back from Darjeeling, and settled down, at around midnight, to my fifth large meal of the day and my second dinner!

The next day I was transported came back to Darjeeling in yet another jeep, the best of the lot, infact a second best to ours! This one was completely open, with not even a pretence of a roof and the road from Sukia Pokri to Ghum is at around 7,000 to 8,000 feet. It was very very cold and I sat on hard wood and am only just beginning to be able to sit down again so sore was my seat by the end. The Tukvar jeep met me in Darjeeling and took me home.

Although the main cart road to Siliguri in the plains lacked some of the excitement of the garden roads, it did have other interests.

Travelled back from Calcutta with just Brigadier Dhilon, the French Consul General and his wife bound for Kalimpong and hardly anyone else on the plane. From the airport I travelled up in the Maharaja of Sikkim's car with two Bengalis and a child sitting behind. Knowing the road and knowing the Bengali's capabilities of being sick I have never spent such an anxious hour. The child was breathing down the back of my neck. Fortunately they got out at Kurseong town half way up.

My mother and the jeep met me in Darjeeling. Mother, the driver and myself sat in the front, behind were four men and a boy a basket 2 1/2 feet high, full of provisions, two geese, my two suitcases and my BOAC bag. The geese, incidentally were alive and every time we went round a goomti [bend] they cackled. It was the first time I had seen the driver smile.

Of all the tea garden roads the Tukvar road was probably the worst, being the steepest. It was a credit to those who drove on these roads that there were few accidents. We were sitting on the veranda of the Planters' Club one day. The 'we' being a group of mostly women since the men had their 'quarterdeck' to retreat to. Not only did the veranda face the snows but from this vantage point one could look down to see who was in town. There was a small car park below and a rickshaw stand. It was usually from here that the planters' wives would leave their cars to walk, often with a lad or a woman with a basket to carry their shopping up the smart shopping streets. Not all the porters were Nepali women, some were Sherpas or Tibetans and wore the traditional striped aprons and big boots.

There was always someone at the Planters' Club, perhaps a pregnant woman waiting for her 'time' because all mothers-to-be were advised to have their babies in Darjeeling now rather than down on the estates, someone convalescing, visitors or planters and their wives up for the day. It was the place to gossip. After sitting there one day I recalled that:

> Some dear old soul told us of a recent car accident when someone had reversed over a bank. She said 'you know the road, a terrible one, you have to reverse on one corner, so silly it should be broadened'. I don't think she realized why we were all in fits of laughter - we have to reverse on nearly every corner on the Tukvar road and such is the steepness of the hill it would be just too big an exercise and too expensive.

And as one travelled through these hills there was the scenery. It was not always hidden in mist and cloud and even when it was, the clouds would sometimes drift away to give an unexpected glimpse of a peak or even the whole of Kanchenjunga before blanketing over again. By moonlight, sunrise, sunset and full daylight the view of Kanchenjunga was always majestic, beautiful and different.

Again we have digressed and must return to those years just after the war, and, in particular, to the 73rd Annual General Meeting of the Darjeeling Planters Association, a branch of the Indian Tea Association. We had left it, if you remember, when the Vice President had recommended that it was time that something was done to improve the roads!

As we stay, for a moment with the subject of roads we will look at what the next speaker had to say. He was Mr. Smyth Osbourne, a man whom I saw as belonging to the past, to the traditions of shikar, and the great days of the NBMR annual camp whereas Malcolm was more of a bridge between the Victorian traditions to those of the mid twentieth century. In 1947 Mr. Smyth Osbourne was still the Manager of Soom, the man who had shot the python and a member of the Bengal Legislative Council. In his address he said:

> Mr. Betten has asked me to speak to you as your representative of the
> Bengal Assembly. During the period I have been in office my main

worries have been Food and Communications... Our group took up, very strongly, the question of building adequate storage godowns. These were built at Darjeeling, Ghum, Kurseong and Siliguri last year; just a year late, they are fine godowns, too; but what has been worrying me is that up to last month there was nothing in them. I am now assured by the authorities that they soon will be full. I shall be very glad to know when that is so. We are at the end of the railway and road. What with the thought of railway and postal strikes, we shall be in a mess unless we have at least four months supply of food (for the labour) in hand.

This brings me to communications which I consider to be very precarious. Our main roads are in a bad way with slips and subsidences. Some years ago I pressed for another outlet for the Darjeeling District and persuaded Government to carry out a survey from the bridge across the Reang near Mirik, up the Mungpo spur to the 3rd mile Simkona. This would be a great assistance to our friends in the Dooars who will have a shorter route to Darjeeling than via Siliguri and Sukna...

I should like to see another outlet for Darjeeling to the plains and suggest to the C. & W. Department that they should survey a motor road from Punkhabri to Kurseong. I believe it would be shorter than the Sukna - Kurseong road. The terrain may be difficult. The portion of the road, Kurseong to Sukna, is the part that is likely to be closed. There is a subsidence below Selim Hill Factory, a subsidence and wash out at Tindharia. A slip at the 13th mile and other subsidences lower down. In my opinion a number of these slips and subsidences are caused by deforestation and all steep slopes above and below the roads which are waste land should be replanted. Under the private property Forest Act Government has powers to make owners plant up waste land and this should be done.

The surface of our roads in the District are bad. In the past the C. & W. Department have made the excuse "no material, no rollers, no labour". In my opinion they should have done more than they have done. One sees coolies picking a hole, in the road and filling it like a tooth being filled but it is never pressed home, as a dentist does when he puts in a filling, and soon rips up. One sees many supervisors, but they do not make sufficient use of the rollers. There is no excuse now as they have modern rollers; but do not use them. More machinery should be used to rip up the old surfaces, and more use should be made of graders, mixers etc. and rollers and last but not least, more careful supervision.

And concerning labour - one hopes that one day, our friends in the Scientific Department will produce a machine to gather leaf. Bone or some plastic scissors which will not damage the shoots and some suction method like a hoover to remove the leaf from the blades...!

As the difficulties of the change to India's Independence approached, Malcolm urged planters to keep their gardens well stocked with provisions, particularly food. There was concern about a possible reduction in the cereal rations 'because the energy of our labour working on these steep mountain slopes, specially during the monsoon period makes it essential that they receive adequate food supplies...'

The centenary of tea in Darjeeling was approaching and the planters were reminded that most estates had a hundred year lease from Government. These would be coming up for renewal in the next few years.

Not only were the leases coming up for renewal but also the bushes, since the commercial life of a bush was about seventy years. The Indian Tea Research Institute had done much good work both in improving productivity and their advice should be heeded and bushes replaced.

Mr. Benton of the Scientific Department was one of the speakers and before I refer to his talk I would ask you to remember that in an earlier chapter reference was made to the original methods of tea manufacture and in particular to the rolling of the leaf into a ball before it was dried. What Mr. Benton had to say in 1947 is, therefore interesting:

All my recent investigations have shown that, in obtaining the greatest profit out of liquor and assortment, rolling is of primary importance, and if the rolling is wrong, no amount of attention to the subsequent states will secure the desired result.

In order to secure the maximum of liquor and flavour, plus the maximum of well twisted grades in the higher categories, a high degree of distortion in all the cells is required, especially in the cells of the stem. This can only be obtained in a roller which is twisting the leaf instead of breaking it and the most important factor is to use a charge of leaf in the roller which will enable the machine to work efficiently.

There seems to be some doubt as to what I am after in rolling, and various schemes of short rolls, few rolls, light pressure, no pressure etc. have been attributed to me. What is actually required is a charge of leaf small enough to allow the roller to work efficiently, and the rolling system will then depend on the rollers and kutcha sifters available.

New telephone pole for Tukvar, 1947

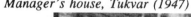

Manager's house, Tukvar (1947)

The tea bush nursery (1950)

Also to speak at the AGM was the Civil Surgeon, Major Brebner of the Indian Medical Service. It is reported that he had not been invited but had requested that he speak to the meeting for he had much to say on health, particularly on the increase of pulmonary tuberculosis among the labour. He urged that small isolation wards be set up on gardens to prevent the spread of the disease.

Before reporting what he had to say on hospitals I would also remind the reader of the Eden Sanatorium which was opened in 1883 for Europeans only and the Lowis Jubilee Sanatorium opened in 1888 for Asians, but with special rates for Hindus. In his talk to the planters in 1946 Major Brebner made the following suggestion:

> I appeal to you to put aside sentiment and memories of the past and do a little thinking about facts. What you should be interested in is the best in first class accommodation for all communities. An Eden wing with the present Victoria Hospital would make one of the best equipped hospitals in India, and the cost to the patient, as far as you are concerned, would be definitely less than it has been to-date.

And as always the day of the AGM closed with a dance, the biggest gathering of local planters in a year. It was a day when the town was full of planters and their wives, even those who usually preferred to stay quietly down on the garden.

With the Independence of India came, as we all know, Partition. Darjeeling was not particularly involved in the Hindu and Muslim riots but the result of the split was a big break in the communications with Calcutta and the outside world, since that part of Pakistan which is now Bangladesh, lies on the direct overland route between Darjeeling and Calcutta. For the traveller to and from Darjeeling, the journey was only simple if one went by air, thus avoiding a long detour and a trip through two lots of Customs.

There is something almost reminiscent of Hooker's journey or Captain Hawthorn's guide in the following extract from one of my letters:

> We arrived just before Bernie and Pinkie, the assistant at Singla, they had just returned from their holiday. They had motored to Calcutta, a three day job, which means being rowed across the Ganges because there is no road bridge. On the outward bound trip they had had to spend two nights in their car perched at an angle on top of a goods railway wagon waiting to cross the river. I am sure that all that was needed was a good bribe?

Independence or no, business, whether in the bazaar or on the tea estates, had to carry on if men are to earn their living. On the tea estates it was business as usual with a day, for the planter, which would probably begin at 6 am in the office.

Grace speaks of the general pattern of life for a planter who so often was depicted as a man with bare knees, a walking stick, a pruning knife and a funny hat.

Sometimes there would be a kind of court case first - someone had lost his wife or someone else's had been stolen and all this court took place outside the office. Big things, murders and so on the police had to do but small, day to day grouses was the manager's job. Then he saw the munshis about the day's work and about 9 o'clock he came in for breakfast.

After breakfast he would go round the garden, walking down in the hills and riding up where it was not possible to take a jeep. Then about 12 - 1 p.m. he would come in, perhaps have a bath then, certainly have lunch, followed by an hour's siesta and then back to work till about six o'clock, perhaps with a break for 'afternoon tea'. The afternoons were usually spent in the office for as well as the job of producing the tea the manager had to work on the welfare of his labour, who required provisions, new cloth, even for the Pujas. Sometimes the managers felt that they were just bazaar wallahs.

Every garden had a hospital and a school and some gardens had a church because in some of the gardens there would probably be several Christians. Life was hard for everyone. The labour were given good accommodation, land for their vegetables and 'guaranteed' employment. Not pleasant in the rains, but they were people of the monsoon and with no rights to any land they had a good, worry free livelihood on the estates. They were free to find better employment, and that they didn't, suggests that there was none.

The rains was a very very busy time, in the hills rainfall varies from garden to garden but in four months, bridges and roads were often washed away and needed to be repaired. No matter how wet, everyone's livelihood depended on the bushes being plucked. All the bushes on the garden were plucked in rotation and the leaf taken, every day to the factory where it was weighed and the manufacturing process of withering begun. This first withering stage of manufacture would depend on the amount of water in the tea. The factory worked night and day and never stopped during the rains. Sometimes managers might take an evening out, perhaps go to another bungalow but often such an evening would end with a walk through the factory at two or three in the morning to check that all was well. The manager would often get up at odd times during the night too, to go into the factory to make sure it was working.

The rains was the time when the tea was made, boxed and stored, because often it could not be got away until after the dry weather. [Because of the ropeway at Tukvar this was less of a problem there.] In the cold weather the tea chests were transported to the countries world wide. Some gardens even experimented with brick tea as the manager of Soom in 1915 records, "A small quantity of brick tea was made for Tibet during the season. The quality was well reported on from Lhasa and an order of 50 maunds received from there and half of this quantity supplied."

During the 'winter' all the tea bushes had to be pruned down to a flat table top level so that the coolies can pluck easily and the bush spreads out to cover the ground, preventing both moisture loss and weeds.

It was a tea tree which was found growing wild in Assam; a tea 'bush' in its natural state will grow to 20/30 feet and those are called bearers which they keep specially for seed. Also a lot of humus is made and put onto the ground and the cultivation done during the cold weather.

In the factory, machinery is all taken to pieces and cleaned and all repaired and new parts added.

But in the cold weather the pressure is off, there is time for holidays, for relaxation and tennis, shooting or fishing.

And always from one year's end to the next, the unpredictable giants rule and the beauty and the scenery remain the same as described by the landscape painter Edward Lear on his visit to Darjeeling in 1874.

January 17. Hard mattress; back bad. Bed miserably uncomfortable but for Giorgio putting it tolerably right. He has a small backroom, cold, but with large fire. Could not get tea till 7.20. Up on hill at once. Wonderful, wonderful view of Kinchinjunga.

20

The Sun Sets on British Sikkim

At India's Independence in 1947, the British in Darjeeling reluctantly, but obediently, accepted that the area had been handed over to the Indian Government. But there was one night, perhaps at the party of their last AGM, before Independence, when a group of planters stayed on late, drinking and talking about 'British Sikkim', the Sikkim Raja's gift to the British and the good old days. They felt that Darjeeling should not be handed over to India but remain British territory and plotted to create an independent state. Those who were serious saw it as a kind of Switzerland, others more fantastically as a Pimlico as depicted in the film 'Passport to Pimlico'.

The plans, which never became public, did get to a sufficiently advanced stage for there to be talk of building an airstrip where Thurbo had a football pitch. The state would survive on tea and tourism but there would be scope for craft industries. The plan remained underground or got left behind with the empty whisky glasses.

The Nepalese were not so tractable. In 1947 the Gurkha or Nepalese League, was formed. While I was there a major strike on the tea estates took place which was more anti-authority than anti-management. Strike was the euphemistic name given to the unnerving action. It was not for nothing that British Sikkim had enjoyed privileges within Bengal, but then British Sikkim had belonged to Sikkim and not to Nepal. The Nepalese living in Darjeeling were (like all but a handful of Lepchas), immigrants in search of a livelihood.

At Independence the British tea planters did not, like the civil servants, leave at once. There had always been some Indian owners and managers but it was more than a decade before Indians had taken control of the majority of the tea estates. I have used the word Indian lightly because one or two gardens belonged to the MacDonalds, the half-Tibetan family from the Kalimpong Hotel.

The Darjeeling I returned to in 1954 was no longer part of Calcutta's social scene although the Governor of Bengal still entertained at Government House with scarlet clad footmen standing behind each guest's chair. Change was most noticeable at the Gymkhana Club. In the 1950s it stood a decaying monument to a bygone era with lights dimmed and paint brown and dismal and with each month that passed a bit more paint peeled off the walls.

There were no longer tea dances at the Gymkhana Club and even the occasional evening dance was poorly attended. There was one occasion, however, when dance floor was full, it was the night the successful British team to climb Kanchenjunga was in town. The planters saw this as a British success, a British night and every tea planter came in to celebrate. I never saw so many planters as gathered that night at the Planters Club for the cocktail party which they gave to the climbers. Even my father's young Scottish assistant who normally touched not a drop of alcohol was there; when he discovered that the price of his ticket was the cost of a bottle of whisky whether he drank it or no, he sat himself in a corner and steadily drank the required number of glasses to be sure he paid for no-one else's enjoyment. He was due to lunch with us the following day - to his credit he was only half a minute late, having walked more than 2,000 feet down the mountainside from his bungalow!

The successful expedition members and the planters then went on to try out their paces on the Gymkhana Club dance floor. This was a large floor with surrounding balcony for those who wished to sit out and watch. Usually just a ghost of its former self, it came to life that night as the Gurkha Officers and the masters of St. Paul's School from Jalapahar joined the planters along with every other Brit in town.

The night was like the last flicker of a candle, for the brown Victorian elegance of the Gym Club had become a morgue, a shell for memories. The roller skating rink, the dining room and the tea lounge were as often as not deserted.

Apart from the ballroom with its spectator gallery and memory of fantastic Christmas parties for the children, the skating rink must hold the most memories for me, and perhaps for others. We had all skated here in our time. In the evening the band played. It was once the custom for liveried men drawing rickshaws to arrive carrying the Governor of Bengal and his entourage. The Governor was an expert and when he arrived to skate others moved aside, not just to give him polite space but to watch his expertise. When, however, the man called Gangooly arrived, everyone, Governor included, stood aside to watch.

In 1954 the best entertainment I could usually find was to join one or two others for one of the club's excellent curries in the empty dining room.

Outside on the tennis courts it was no better. The Tibetan, Gyelo Thondup, His Highness, the Dalai Lama's brother, was the only regular player. The courts, surrounded by rusty and empty spectator stands were silent as the Marker of the Tennis Courts played with Thondup. Thondup was strong, fit and sad, a man who was waiting, preparing for the future. I was happy to stand and watch him and the Marker play as the world waited for the next sad chapter of history to unfold.

As we say our farewells to the town of Darjeeling, the sun is again shining on the Kanchenjunga snows and to the east we can see the Jelep la. Before leaving the District let us go down to the emerald Teesta and, crossing the waterfall which tumbles down the hillside to flow under and sometimes over the road, climb up the hill to Kalimpong. This land was once taken from Sikkim by Bhutan and then added to Darjeeling District by the British after a skirmish with the Bhutanese.

A gathering of some Darjeeling personalities in 1953, including Bishop Bryan, Leslie Goddard, Padre Duncan, Jim Duncan (Kalimpong Homes Superintendent) and Molly his wife, Daisy Fowles of KH, Angtharkay, Tenzing and Ang Lahmu his wife

Described by some as the prettiest hill station in the Darjeeling District and possibly in India, Kalimpong is as different from Darjeeling as chalk is from cheese. Never a resort for the Calcutta fashionable, it was able to develop its own identity as an international hill town attracting peoples from all parts of the world. I learned to love this town where all the tribes and religious of Asia meet. It was like a busy port where all sorts meet at a street corner to gossip, exchange news and business. Instead of ships coming in from the sea, mule train after mule train, bells tinkling, loads swaying, staggered in from the distant Tibetan plateau. On Saturdays Kalimpong's colourful bazaar has a Central Asian atmosphere. The gateway to Tibet, home of scholars and a centre of Buddhism; living in Kalimpong was a rare experience.

In 1950, before I had come to Kalimpong His Holiness the Dalai Lama had included a visit to Kalimpong on his trip to India because he felt that he had a spiritual duty to visit his fellow countrymen.

While at Kalimpong His Holiness wrote to the United Nations, hoping for help in his conflict with the Chinese, but nothing came of it. Matters had reached such a pitch that in 1959 the Dalai Lama fled over the passes to Tezpur and thousands of his countrymen followed him, flocking to Tezpur and on to Dharmsala, but also to Darjeeling and Kalimpong.

The troubles of Tibet seemed a long way away, when in 1954, in the serenity of the beautiful Kalimpong flower gardens I strolled with the beautiful young princesses of both Sikkim and Bhutan, who along with Tinkabell, a Tibetan princess, had visited Dr. Graham's Homes. Living here, in Kalimpong as he had done, the founder of these Homes had been friends with their grandfathers. A remarkable and international man, it is difficult to assess the full contribution of Dr. Graham, to both the Homes and to Kalimpong town. He founded these Homes at the end of the nineteenth century, for destitute Anglo Indians and they had grown in size to become a town within a town. The school took in some fee paying children and even during the months that I worked there, was getting requests to take Tibetan children. There was nothing surprising about this because Dr. Graham had always looked outwards from the Homes towards the neighbouring hill states. The following is an extract from the Homes' Magazine at the time of Dr. Graham's death.

Until he was of advanced age he travelled widely in Bhutan, Sikkim, Nepal and Tibet. He had the closest ties perhaps with Bhutan. He loved the country and its rulers. His contact with Bhutan flourished and grew due to his friendship with Bhutanese nobleman, Raja Ugyen Dorji, who acted as Agent for Bhutan to the British Government. Graham and he were friends for 27 years.

In 1922 he was invited into Bhutan by the then Maharajah to make suggestions as to how the country could be developed and modern-

164

ised... and was awarded the Bhutan Gold medal for his services to Bhutan.

However, one of his most interesting letters was written to the Dalai Lama, (his holiness's predecessor) drawing His Holiness's attention to the bad state of the road at the Jelap La pass which was dangerous for mules. He says he knows His Holiness's interest in animals and is sure that he will arrange for the road to be repaired.

This missionary who was, in so many ways, not just the father of the Homes, but also of Kalimpong, died in 1942 and the roads in Kalimpong were jammed as thousands attended his funeral, Christians, Buddhists, Hindus and Muslims all came to mourn.

For most of 1955 I stayed with, and worked for, the Superintendent of Dr. Graham's Homes, Kalimpong, the Rev. Jim Duncan and Molly his wife. Jim was the son of the padre who had written the Nepalese dictionary.

My first letter from Kalimpong records that:

Tea is at 3.30 and we were just finishing tea on Wednesday, my first day, when Prince Peter of Greece and Denmark arrived, he is a cousin of the Duke of Edinburgh and is tall and handsome with an airforce moustache and an infectious laugh. He is very interesting and at the moment is writing a book about the race of Tibetans.

He says that from his point of view it is better than being in Tibet as Tibetans come to Kalimpong from all corners of Tibet and have to register with the police and are given a pass. At the moment I understand that 30,000 Tibetans are registered here a year. Prince Peter at the moment is very busy measuring them. He does it by working with the police and measuring them as they come to be registered. Although the police take their fingerprints, this they do by making the Tibetans dip their fingers, all of them, in some black stuff, until recently, before they were given a cloth, they would clean their hands by rubbing them on the wall!

Kalimpong was a bridge between the West, India and Tibet and, while I was there, secret and scaring news was filtering through to those concerned of atrocities and problems which were to culminate in the arrival of thousands of Tibetans, fleeing from the Chinese. The arrival of the Tibetan refugees opens a new book and closes the pages of this one.

As the sun finally sets over the snowy mountains, and British Sikkim takes its place in history, I close with some extracts from 'My Life and my Hopes' an essay by the Tibetan, Dawa Norbu, when in Class XI at the Kalimpong Homes:

The last decade has opened a special chapter in my life. The perils and ordeals that filled my childhood, and the slice of luck that steered the course of my life into happiness and education shall never be forgotton.

....I was then ten years old when we made a miraculous escape to India. Young as I was, I can recollect every detail of that exacting episode. I remember every moment of that hazardous journey. Having arrived safely at Gangtok, we decided to go to Darjeeling... Thus, it was more from economic reasons than academic that one wintry day in 1962 my mother took me to a 'school', then a mere camp for refugee children in Darjeeling, but now a proper school.

Later Dawa Norbu was to be sponsored and was able to go to the school at Dr. Graham's Homes, Kalimpong before going on to higher education.
...The Homes has made me into 'a new man', superstitions are substituted by science, and false beliefs by logic and reason. But at the same time I am not iconoclastic. I preserve my Tibetan identity...

I cherish a sincere hope that by the wise counsel and positive actions of our fellowmen, and by the utmost endeavour of the Tibetans in exile to be 'not independent but interdependent' in their freedom struggle, Tibet will become free again. I also hope for a new Democratic Tibet as declared by H. H. The Dalai Lama, a land where truth and justice prevail, a land where the ancient culture of Tibet and modern civilisation will exist side by side. Above all I hope that I may become one of the architects of the Tibet of my dream, contributing all that I have acquired from Dr. Graham's Homes, my second home.

Eva Betten and author at Lebong races (1954)

166